Surviving the Wild:

*A Girlfriend's Guide to Surviving
High School*

contents:

Dedicated to Heather and David Bokowy.

Thank you for your endless guidance, love, support, and forgiveness. I could not have asked for better parents. I love you both with my whole heart. Here's to redemption and second chances!

For girls, everywhere. May you live in the freedom of a life lived with the Father.

Acknowledgements

This book would not have been possible were it not for the help of several people. Left up to my own devices, this book would never have happened.

I want to thank Susan Jenkins for not only her editing expertise, but her constant love and encouragement throughout this whole process. Mama Jenkins, I love you dearly! Second I wish to thank Jennifer Walker for not only being my mentor this past year, but also for helping me change the view I had of myself my junior year of high school. Thank you for encouraging me to believe that the Lord delights in me and that I am His. You mean more to me and my family than you will ever know. Holly Sharp, thank you for your last-minute agreement to help me make this book the greatest it can be. You are a life saver! Hailey Chapman, thank you for being the artist willing to design the cover of this book for me and for being my constant encouragement and friend. I love you more than words can describe. Crystal Earle, thank you for being my go to woman this past year. Thank you for believing in me and reminding me everything is going to be okay. Ryan Stone, thank you for the way you took me under your wing my freshman year and continued to encourage me all four years of high school. I can't wait for you to follow me on Twitter, dude! To my mother, Heather Bokowy, who came up with the idea for this book, you are the greatest and I am so thankful for who you are. Thank you for continuing to pursue me and care for me each and every day. If I am even half the woman you are when I grow up I will consider myself lucky. To my father, David Bokowy, thank you for never failing to encourage me and pursue me with the Lord's love. Thank you for showing me, my whole life, what a man of God looks like. I hope to find one like you one day.

Finally, to the middle and high school girls who helped me write this book and were willing to share their lives with me, I thank you. Without you, this would not have been possible. I loved getting to share my story with you all, and having a piece of your story in the pages of this book, makes it even more special. This book is for you!

Introduction

A Note from the Author

Bob Goff says in his best-selling book Love Does, "Most people need love and acceptance a lot more than they need advice." I chose to write A Girlfriend's Guide to Surviving High School because I firmly believe what Bob Goff is trying to convey. My transition from middle school to high school was nothing short of disaster and I wanted a means of documenting that journey in a way that was beneficial to others. I have known for a long time that I have wanted to do this, and I had to seize the opportunity when it presented itself. I wanted to use my past experiences in order to assist girls through this life transition called adolescence. High school is a journey filled with a lot of joy and a lot of confusion. I will be the first to admit that I wanted my high school years to look exactly like they did in my favorite TV show, One Tree Hill. I will also be the first to admit that my hopes were definitely unrealistic. I believe that the media world has given young girls a distorted view of high school and all of its aspects. My hope and my prayer for the girls who read this book is that they will be able to connect to my story in some way and learn from my mistakes. This book is written from a biblical perspective because my relationship with the Lord is very important to me and is a huge part of my story. I hope that my book and my experience will become a guide for middle school girls transitioning to high school. I pray that the girls who pick up my book will never struggle like I did. I pray that, just like Bob Goff said, my book becomes not only advice but the love and acceptance girls look for as they struggle in adolescence.

Before You Read...

For starters, welcome to your guide to surviving high school!! I am so very glad you have decided to pick up this book and embark on this journey with me. I am so glad you are here! I pray that this book will be beneficial to you and has tangible lessons which you can carry on to your high school years. I know for me, my transition from middle school to high school was not a fun one. Even some of the first years I spent in high school were not fun as I continued to journey through adolescence. This book is comprised of seven chapters all focusing on different topics that I struggled with during my transition from middle school to high school. Within each chapter, you will see evidence of interviews I had with real middle school girls. I met with girls from public, private and charter schools within my hometown. I asked that they fill out a questionnaire at the end of our time together that I created based on the topics about which I was writing. You will also see evidence of interviews I had with high school girls, from public, private, and charter schools, within my hometown. I tweaked the questionnaire a little bit and focused theirs more on their past experiences in high school. With the middle school girls' questionnaire, I had most of those questions future focused, meaning I asked them what they expected high school to be like and what they were hopeful for or nervous about moving forward.

There are a few specific things I wanted to touch on before you begin this book. The first being, my relationship with the Lord. This is very important to me and I firmly believe that Jesus is the only reason I am where I am today. I talk about Him quite a lot through the course of this book and I refer to scripture a good amount because I know for a fact, I do not have all of the answers. If you are not a fan of learning from scripture or from another's relationship with the Lord, this book probably is not for you. Secondly, there are a few terms I mention frequently throughout this book. Some of these may not be common knowledge, and I wanted to explain them!

The first "term" I believe I need to explain is a charter school. I currently attend a charter high school in Greenville, South Carolina and I had the opportunity to meet with middle and high school girls who attend charter schools and use their responses within this book. First of all, a charter school is not a private school. That is a common misconception made by many people. A charter school is a school that is, most of the time, started by parents but still receives government funding. The parents, or community leaders, responsible for starting the school come up with a "charter" that establishes who they wish the school to be and what they wish to accomplish. If the charter is passed by the state government, the school receives funding but is able to operate on the regulations set in the charter. My high school has been such a blessing to me and I am so thankful a group of parents decided to create it.

The second thing I want to go briefly over with you is Jack. You will hear me reference the name Jack a good amount through the pages of this book. Jack was my first boyfriend and played a huge role in my life for about five years. Our relationship revolved around deceit and lies all five years. We lied to my parents about the seriousness of our relationship from the get go. During the ending years of our relationship I discovered he was never faithful to me and just about everything he told me was a lie. Finding this out left a lasting mark on my heart and my self-esteem. Coming out of that relationship, I was wounded and hurt in more ways than I can describe. He left a mark on me and my story like no other. However, the Lord used this situation for His glory and my redemption in the end, which you will shortly see!

The third is Young Life. Now, you are probably thinking, "What is Young Life?" Well, Young Life is a non-profit outreach ministry devoted to sharing the love of Jesus with middle school and high school students. Now, why is this important? My dad has been on Young Life staff for 25 years now. I have grown up with the privilege of watching him share the Gospel with high school students every day. I also had the privilege of being a part of this ministry during my high school years. I reference Young Life quite a lot throughout this book because it has played such an important role in my life.

The fourth thing I mention frequently is my immediate family! I live with my two parents, Heather and David, and my wonderful little brother, Ryan. As I said earlier, my dad has worked with Young Life for 25 years.

My dad is the wisest person I know. He has the ability to bring people together like no one I have ever seen. He is such a leader and cares for other people so well. He is hilarious and always knows how to make me laugh. My mom is a licensed professional counselor. She is the kindest person I know. She loves the people around her so well and is one of the best influences in my life. She challenges others to be their very best and encourages them to do so with everything she has. My brother is the sweetest person I know. He has such a kind spirit and is so, so sweet. I love all three of them very much and each one of them has played a significant role in my life. I wanted to introduce you to them before we get going here!

Finally, to protect the privacy of the individuals mentioned from my past, names have been changed unless otherwise noted.

As you journey through the pages of this book, I hope you can remember that your story is yours alone. No one else can tell you how to live your high school years. Whether you like it or not, you will be faced with a multitude of new decisions to make as you enter this new chapter of your life. Is it scary and at times confusing? Yes, I will not lie to you. However, I have great news for you. You are not alone. You never have been and you never will be. The One who created you has chosen to walk this journey with you. He is by your side and he will never ever leave you, no matter how hard high school gets, and no matter how scary it may seem. Deuteronomy 31:6 says, "Be strong and courageous. Do not be afraid or terrified because of them, for the Lord your God goes with you; he will never leave you nor forsake you." I could not say anything better than that! Girlfriends, let's dive into this journey together. Grab your gear, it's time to go survive high school and kick its butt!!

1

Too Cool for School?

Work THEN Play

Schoolwork is hard in high school, man. I am not going to sugar coat it for you. Arithmetic becomes Algebra and Pre-Calculus. Reviewing vocab words becomes 4 page essays. Science classes become more advanced and before you know it you're dissecting pigs. Study hall will soon become your best friend and your teacher's office hours will become your safe place. I know this is not what anyone wants to hear but here is the fact of the matter; according to the state and to your parents, your full-time job, while in high school, is to be a student. Now, you're probably thinking one of these two things: "I am going to be completely organized in high school. I will never fall behind and I will always turn things in early." Or you may be thinking, "Who cares? High school is just the beginning of another grade closer to me getting out of school." Both of these options are wrong. For the girl who believes she can stay super up-to-date and never fall behind, I'm sorry but you will fail at some point. You will, at some point, forget you have a grammar worksheet due in English II. We are all flawed humans and not a single one of us is perfect. Now, for the girl who doesn't care about school and just wants to get by, you are pushing your luck. Unfortunately, our society runs on young professionals with college degrees. You happen to get to college by first graduating high school. I am a senior in high school this year and I am going to let you in on a little secret...the Algebra I final exam that I failed at the end of freshman year is reflected quite nicely on my high school transcript. That is an important fact to have in the back of your mind. I know when I was a freshman I did not realize that everything started to mean so much. Now I am applying to colleges and they are looking at all of high school and what my grades looked like all four years. Your senior year is not the only year that matters. I say this not to scare you. I say this to prepare you. The more prepared you are the more successful you will be in the end.

Going from middle school homework to high school homework was definitely a wake-up call for me. I have never been the kind of student who can get all A's without studying. My brother, however, is that person. (Still bitter about that) I have always had to work really hard for my grades. Math is not my thing. I will be real, I believe Satan himself created math. However, if you ask me to write an essay, I will kill it! One of the biggest things I have realized is that in order to succeed you need to give your work your all. Why would you do a job if you are not going to give it your best?

> ## Describe your ideal "studying situation"
>
> "I (need) lots of Quizlets because I love Quizlet. I can't do memorization and I can't sit down and study for long periods of time!"
>
> **Nora - 8th Grader**

Back in Jesus' day, school definitely looked different than it does today. Therefore, He does not leave clear instructions for how schoolwork is to be done. However, He tells us, through King Solomon, in Proverbs 14:23, "All hard work brings a profit, but mere talk leads only to poverty." As I mentioned earlier, your full-time job at this point in your life is to be a student. Being a student is hard work. Keeping up with your grades is hard work. Trying to make good decisions is hard work. Girl, I am right there with you! Here is some great news for you, Genesis 2:3 says, "And God blessed the seventh day and made it holy, because on it he rested from all the work of creating that he had done." The Lord knows what hard work feels like. He understands that rest is an important activity we need. That is why he created Sunday. Now, I understand that your work comes before your play. However, you need to make sure that you are allowing yourself time to rest and enjoy high school. Read this list of ideas:

~ Plan a day trip to the nearest outlet mall with your mom.

~ Have a movie night with your best friend.

~ Have a family game night.

~ Go out to eat to your favorite restaurant with a group of friends.

~ Plan to make dinner at home with a group of friends.

~ Plan to go to a movie you've been wanting to see for a while.

~ Go on a date night with your dad.

~ Take an hour-long bath with some fun soap and bath bombs.

~ Cook/bake your favorite snack or dessert.

Once you have read the list, number the list 1 to 10; 1 being the first activity you wish to do and 10 being the least fun idea to you. You now have a list of 10 things you can do, one per week, on a weekend, once your homework is completed! 10 activities, one per week, equals 10 weeks. If you happen to have a mountain of homework one weekend, push your activity to the next week. This is a great way to get you started with taking care of yourself and giving yourself room to rest.

Finding a balance of schoolwork and fun during high school is difficult. Take it from me; I'm dealing with it right this moment. In high school, activities become more fun, you are given more freedom, and your number one desire most definitely does not consist of sitting at your kitchen table doing schoolwork all day. However, even though you acquire more freedom socially, more responsibility will come academically. Your grades are vitally important from day one of your freshman year to day 180 of your senior year. Find a balance. Try not to consume your life with so much schoolwork that you forget to have a little fun every now and then. Try not to have so much fun that you forget about all your assignments that are due Monday morning. Life is not black and white like that. Have fun and enjoy your high school years but remember to get the not-so-fun things (AKA schoolwork) out of the way first! Girl, call me when you finish that paper that's due on Monday! I'd love to get coffee with you.

The SAT from Satan

I will never forget the number 980. You're probably thinking that seems like a strange number to remember. You are right. Do you want to take a guess on what that number represents? Yep. My first two SAT scores. Now, if you are a freshman, you probably are not even thinking about this test yet. If you are a sophomore, you are probably still not thinking about this yet. If you are a junior, you probably are beginning to prepare for this. If you are a senior, you know the drill. Let me give you a little bit of an explanation here. The highest score on the SAT (as of March 2016) is a 1600. The lowest score is a 400. Most colleges have a bare minimum score requirement of 1000. That is the absolute bare minimum. Half of the time, they really want you to at least get a 1200. You saw my test score. I told you about the requirements of colleges. How do you think I felt when I received my score? I can tell you if you'd like. I was defeated, discouraged, anxious and down-right pissed off. I took the SAT a second time and I received a 980 again. There was no change to my score whatsoever. I took the SAT a third time, after 8 weeks of tutoring going through an entire SAT prep workbook, and I made a 940. I really did not have words when I saw that third score. I was so angry. I could not figure out what I had done wrong or what I could have improved.

My junior year of high school, I decided that my dream college would be The University of Tennessee in Knoxville (UTK). I had visited twice at the time I decided this. The first time I visited with my mom. We took an official tour and I absolutely fell in love. The second time, I went with my dad and we went to a tailgate party that the Admissions Office was throwing for all prospective students. We attended the event and then went to the football game in Neyland Stadium. I fell in love with the school all over again. I remember opening the letter that told me my application was being put under secondary review. I, of course, read the letter as a straight up "no." My parents reassured me that this was a great opportunity for me to show them just how much I want to attend

UTK. I called the admissions counselor, Doug Smith, responsible for North and South Carolina applicants the next day. He said thirteen words that shattered my confidence. "If it wasn't for your test scores, I would admit you this moment." What the heck, dude??? I was so hurt and confused. Mr. Smith told me that the rest of my application was "superb." Everything except for my test scores was just where it needed to be for me to be admitted. Mr. Smith encouraged me to take the SAT one more time in January and send those scores as quickly as possible to their office.

I could have walked away from this conversation one of two ways. I could have said, "Well that's it, I give up. My score is never going to improve so why does it matter?" Or I could have said, "This is a great opportunity for me to work my tail off and try to improve that score as much as humanly possible. The rest is up to the Lord." I struggled for a very long time to believe that retaking the test was even worth the time and effort to achieve the score I needed. I called a tutor and met with her twice a week for 4 weeks before my test. I bought one of those huge SAT prep books and I did 20 pages a day. By test day, I had completed the entire math portion of the prep book. I walked into the test confident and I took the test for the last time...

> *If you could leave a word of advice to a middle school girl about preparing for standardized testing what would it be?*
>
> "Study! Take your time! Take it one question at a time and don't get overwhelmed!"
>
> **Kendra - High School Senior**

Until I received my score back, I called my friend, Doug Smith, just about every day for six weeks. I would come up with random questions to ask him and hope he wouldn't hang up on me as soon as I said, "Hey Mr. Smith, it's Megan Bokowy calling again..." The week before I got my score back I received the best news. My friend, Kaytlin, was stupid and decided to try and give herself a dreadlock in her beautiful, long, curly hair. Kaytlin was in our school's pageant the next day so she was modeling her formal gown for me in her living room when she realized halfway through the process that things were not going to work out in her favor if she kept this dread going. (Just a disclaimer here, the fact that Kaytlin was getting a dread in her hair was not the good news I was talking about earlier. Just sit tight.) I was helping her shampoo the dread out of her hair when I heard my phone buzz. Just to give you a visual on the situation, the two of us were in a tiny hall bathroom, Kaytlin's head was in the sink, she was still wearing her formal gown and my hands were covered in shampoo and Kaytlin's curls. I looked down at my phone's lock screen long enough to see that I had a new email. The email was from the University of Tennessee and the first words I read were, "Congratulations, you're a Vol!" I screamed in excitement and threw my hands in the air. Little did I remember that my hands were still tangled in Kaytlin's hair so when I threw my hands, the dread came with it. Yes. I yanked the dread right out. We didn't even realize what had just happened until I looked down and found a chunk of her hair in the palm of my hands. We laughed out loud and then cried together because of the news that I had just received! However, I had not received my final score back yet and I hadn't sent it to any schools. How did this happen, you may ask? Because of the perseverance and countless phone calls I had made to my best friend, Doug Smith, they saw that I really, really, really wanted to go to their school and, thankfully, that mattered more than a silly test score. The long-awaited letter of acceptance had finally come and I could not have been happier in that moment

I tell you this story to show you two things: standardized testing is the worst (for poor test takers like myself) and that faithfulness and perseverance both pay off in the end. Standardized tests, whether it be the ACT or SAT, are hard tests. They are designed to be hard tests. They are designed to trick you and scare you. Testing is not my thing at all. I overthink most of the questions and I get super anxious in a testing environment. If you are a good test taker and your scores are where they need to be, more power to you! I am proud of you and you need to keep up the great work. However, there are girls like me who are poor test takers. For those of you, like me, I commend you as well. Keep up the good work. Accept help and never forget that your worth is not found in an ACT or SAT number, no matter what colleges may tell you or how they may treat you. Philippians 4:13 says, "I can do all things through him who gives me strength." All things! You will fail, at times, because the world we live in is broken, and nothing is perfect. However, you can have the confidence to take that test with the peace that He is on your side and He is rooting for you! And just so you know, my final score made it over 1000. It was a great day!

Secondly, I want you to understand the importance of faithfulness and perseverance. Sometimes you have to call the admissions office practically every day for six weeks begging for them to let you into their school. Sometimes that may just do the trick but sometimes it won't. One of my good friends Jim wanted to go to Ohio State University for as long as I've known him. He had worked so hard on his essay and application requirements only to find out that he had been denied acceptance. He tried calling and begged them to reconsider their decision. They wouldn't. Jim was heartbroken and unsure of where he would end up. In situations like these where our efforts seem to do no good, the Lord is still faithful. Alex was accepted into his second-choice school and will be attending there in the fall with some of our other good friends! The Lord doesn't promise us an easy life. The Lord doesn't promise us that our efforts will be noticed all the time. Sometimes you get into the school of your dreams and sometimes we get into our second-choice university.

Romans 8:28 tells us, "And we know that in all things God works for the good of those who love him, who have been called according to his purpose." I'm sure you can think of a thousand things that you feel would make your life complete. I am going to let you in on a little secret here... Nothing can compare to what Jesus has in store for your life. The things you can think of are things of this world. The things Jesus has in store for you are eternal things He is going to use for His purposes in your life. Paul writes to us in the book of Philippians. Philippians 1:19 says, "For I know that through your prayers and God's provision of the Spirit of Jesus Christ what has happened to me will turn out for my deliverance." Here is a fun fact for you. Paul was in jail when he wrote Philippians. Jail. He was in jail and he still had this kind of optimism. He had this optimism because he knew who was on his side through every situation. I had to continually remember this passage while I was working through my SAT prep book. Paul was in jail for sharing the Gospel with others and he had the courage to trust the Lord and His plan despite the circumstances. Sometimes we have to do that. Sometimes we have to find the courage to believe that the Lord has our best interests at heart and no matter the grade on your Algebra II test, no matter the SAT or ACT score you receive, and no matter the colleges you end up getting into, He has got your back and He is cheering for you! If you can picture Jesus literally cheering for you in the front of that room while you take the SAT or ACT it will dramatically change how you take that test. I promise you He is cheering and in all honesty ladies, He probably made a sign!

Study Buddy Central

Study buddies can be a great thing or an awful thing. In my experience, studying with a friend has proven to be very helpful. In studying with a friend, you get the opportunity to learn from each other. Say you are an English person but your typical study buddy is a Math person. You both have an essay due and an Algebra II test to take at some point in the next week. Because you are studying together, you both get the opportunity to help each other with both the essay and the studying. Say your friend is really struggling with the intro paragraph of her essay. You happen to be struggling to understand factorials in your Algebra II class. You two can easily divide and conquer in this moment of academic stress. You can review your friend's essay and see if you two can come up with a killer intro paragraph. Meanwhile, your friend can look at your Algebra II worksheet and see if she can figure out where you went wrong on question 16.

My best friend Kaytlin and I spent every Wednesday night before our Thursday Biology tests together in the fall of 2016. Those Wednesday nights were spent eating more food than I care to talk about, singing, having dance parties, life talks, coffee breaks, and studying for our Biology tests that would come to bite us in the butt the next morning. Those nights were some of the greatest. Kaytlin would help me understand the chapters I did not understand and vice versa. We spent our time making flashcards together, reviewing key terms, coming up with different ways to remember things, all while listening to classical guitar music.

Now, before you begin searching for a study partner or second guessing all of your current study habits, you need to decide if learning with other people is a study tactic that is beneficial for you. Everyone studies a different way. No two people are the same. I know you probably know this already, but the Bible does not offer us any verses tailored to today's academic world. God does not tell us if it is a good idea to have a "study buddy" or not. He doesn't tell us how to write that paper. He doesn't tell us how to solve factorials. He does, however, share with us, through David, in Proverbs 27:17 by saying, "As iron sharpens iron, so one person sharpens another."

The visual David is trying to portray in this verse is one of weapon making. Weapon making was a trade in the days of David. One way to sharpen anything made out of iron is to heat it up and smash it with a hammer. Ninety-nine percent of the time that hammer was made of iron as well. This verse refers to a process that was very common during the time of David. Now, the second part of this verse refers to a person "sharpening" another person. This verse could be talking about any aspect of a person's life. For our purposes let's look at it from an academic perspective. Just like I said before, in studying with someone, you have an incredible opportunity to learn from each other. You also have an incredible opportunity to distract each other and accomplish nothing. Finding a balance between the two is key. Kaytlin and I found that balance and we continue to work with each other to this day.

> *If you could leave a word of encouragement to a middle school girl about academics, what would it be?*
>
> "You need to study the way you do best and don't procrastinate!"
>
> Maria - High School Freshman

Ecclesiastes 4:9-10 says, "Two are better than one, because they have a good return for their work: If one falls down, his friend can help him up. But pity the man who falls and has no one to help him up!" We have all felt this way. You just got that test or that paper back. You thought you killed it. Instead of killing it, you murdered it, as in you failed. We have all been there. Ecclesiastes gives us a pretty awesome picture of what a quality study buddy can do for you. I know whenever I get a poor test grade back Kaytlin is always the first person I tell if I am upset. She is always there to reassure me that there is always another test to take and that I have time to improve. Good study buddies study with you just because you two have work you have to finish. Great study buddies spur you on to do your very best and help you every step of the way.

I don't know about you but I have had to see a tutor once or twice in my lifetime. I remember when I first had to start seeing my math tutor I was a little embarrassed, to be honest. I felt like I wasn't good enough. I felt like I wasn't smart enough to do the work I needed to do in order to succeed. Proverbs 12:15 says, "The way of a fool seems right to him, but a wise man listens to advice." For someone who struggles with pride as much as I do, this verse hits home. I believed for a very long time that I did not need to accept help. I believed that I needed to do everything on my own. The fact of the matter is, I couldn't do the math on my own and I needed to accept help. The more I saw dear, old Mrs. Ashmore, the more I learned and the more confident I felt in my ability to do the math.

This idea of not wanting to accept help played itself out in my life in many ways and always ended up being about my pride. Here's the deal friend...sometimes we just can't do it on our own. Sometimes we need to swallow our pride, sit in the chair, and let some old lady help us with our math homework. Sometimes we need to realize that we need help. This struggle with pride has infected all of our lives in many more ways than just with schoolwork. For me, realizing my need for help when it came to math was the most tangible way to pinpoint my struggle with pride. Nobody wants to admit they can't do something. Mrs. Ashmore helped me realize that even though I couldn't do the math currently, I was going to be able to do it eventually. She never failed to remind me that I was not alone in my struggle and she never made me feel less than because of that struggle. There are things in the academic world that we absolutely cannot do on our own. You will realize that eventually. In times like those, call a tutor, suck it up and embrace his or her help. Find yourself a Mrs. Ashmore and you may have found the best study buddy ever!

MY prayers for YOU: Too Cool for School??

To the girl who struggles with schoolwork, I pray the Lord will give you perseverance to make it through the next school day. (Isaiah 40:8)

To the girl who feels like she is "too smart" for her own good, I pray you will be thankful for the brain the Lord has given you. (Ephesians 5:20)

To the girl who is anxious about every test and every project, I pray you will have the Lord's unending peace. (2 Thessalonians 3:16)

To the girl who struggles to accept help in the subjects she does not understand, I pray the Lord will soften your heart and give you a teachable spirit. (I Peter 5:6-7)

To the girl who is terrified to fail in any school work she does, I pray the Lord will take your anxiety away and allow you to not be crippled by it any longer. (Philippians 4:6-7)

This is my beloved charter high school.
Long live the Trailer Park!

My homie and favorite study buddy! My kitchen table looks
like this quite often when I'm with her.

2

Work It, Girl

Why Do We Work?

Working in high school, like most all things, can be a great opportunity. One great question to consider before applying for jobs is why? Why do we, as a culture, work? Many people would say, "You have to provide for your family somehow." A more, simple answer for people your age would just be, "You work to earn money." This is true but in all honesty, we were designed to work from the beginning. Genesis 2:15 says, "The Lord God took the man and put him in the Garden of Eden to work it and take care of it." The Lord created Adam to work and He created the garden to be worked. I feel like there is a misconception about how the only reason we have to work is because of the Fall (The decision Adam and Eve made to disregard the Lord's boundary and eat from the tree He instructed them not to). However, the Fall of mankind does not come into play until Genesis chapter 3! It is not because of the Fall that we have to work. It is because of the Fall that we have gained a distorted view of work. Work is now hard and it is not what it was intended to be in the first place. Before the Fall, Adam worked for the Lord and with the Lord. After the Fall, it became harder and, especially in today's world, we work for the wrong things. Today, people work strictly for the salary, to feel a sense of belonging, and some even make it their identity. John 2:15-17 says, "Do not love the world or anything in the world...For everything in the world—the lust of the flesh, the lust of the eyes, and the pride of life—comes not from the father but from the world. The world and its desires pass away but whoever does the will of God lives forever."

My work experience began with babysitting. I started babysitting when I was about twelve and I continue to do so whenever the opportunity presents itself. Let me tell you something... you can make some darn good money by babysitting. I would highly recommend it as a first job! Anyways, in the fall of my junior year, I began working at CFA. (More commonly known as Chick-Fil-A) I know that working at Chick-Fil-A may seem like a cliché first job for many teenagers. However, let me tell you about my experience before you jump to conclusions. I love working there. I have met some of the best people during my time there. The owner of my store, Bill, is very involved in the store and we see him often. He is quite the guy. He is wealthier than anyone can imagine but he is one of the most down-to-earth people I have ever met. He is so generous with his wealth and is so kind to all of his employees. He loves the Lord and everyone knows that. In the summer after my junior year, Bill pulled me into his office and told me that he saw real leadership potential in me and he would love to watch that grow. He offered me a position on their leadership team and I gladly accepted. Now, like any promotion, I had to earn that position. I was not just given that role. I did not earn that opportunity by just showing up to work and surviving the shift. I feel like a lot of people look at a job in that light. However, when I go to work, I engage with customers and employees alike, I do my job to the best of my ability, and I try my very best to enjoy myself while I am there. My mom has always told me "there is no point in working if you aren't going to give it your all!" Mom is right! (As always.) I will admit to you that every shift is not easy. I get annoyed with customers and I get annoyed with my bosses at times. However, when I look at the bigger picture of my time working there, I feel like I have genuinely made the most of every experience.

I know everyone loves talking about authority so let's touch on that for a second. There are definitely certain managers at Chick-fil-A that I have a hard time with. There have been times where I had to go hide in the cooler in order to keep my mouth shut around those managers. I have had to learn to swallow my pride and accept the fact that my bosses and managers have been placed in authority over me for a reason and it is my responsibility, as an employee, to honor that. (No matter how difficult it may be!) Romans 13:1 says, "Let every person be subject to the governing authorities. For there is no authority except from God, and those that exist have been instituted by God." There you have it, ladies, straight from the Bible. Authority will be a part of any job you take on and I feel like that is something important you need to remember!

Jumping back on the topic of babysitting, this past year, I have been a nanny for this precious five-year-old little girl. Her name is Whitley Grace. I watch Whitley on Wednesday nights so her mom can go to her church's small group. I then come back Thursday afternoon, pick her up from school, go home to get our snack, and then we go to dance. I am not entirely sure what kind of dance five-year-old girls do but it involves a lot of jumping around and falling on the ground. It's actually the cutest thing I have every witnessed. Watching Whitley is the highlight of my week. She is so full of life and sass.

> ## Where would you want to work while in high school, and what are your concerns?
>
> "I would love to work at my horse barn. I am concerned about not having enough time to do homework or hang out with friends."
>
> **Sara - 7th Grader**

My day with Whitley is no easy task. Many people believe that babysitting is the easiest job in the world. That is very possible. However, I've found that putting the kids you're watching in front of the TV for five hours is not the way to do it. I have learned so much about myself from hanging out with Whitley. She may only be five but she has some incredible insights and thoughts about the world. She talks to me about Jesus, her friends at school, and her life at home with her Mommy! Her mom, Becca, has been such a blessing to me. As Becca has shared her story with me about being a single mom and how her situation with Whitley unfolded, I have been able to learn so much through her as well. Being a part of Becca and Whitley's lives has been the biggest blessing to me.

Not all babysitting jobs are bland and boring. Take a leap of faith if you're offered a babysitting job. You may just meet the most incredible little girl with a sweet mamma that you get to hang out with twice a week.

Both of the examples of work I have shared with you are two very different jobs and require very different skills. I remember feeling, for a long time, that I wasn't good at doing anything and I couldn't figure out what I wanted to do with my life. In accepting my job at CFA and working there for almost 2 years now, I have realized that I do not want to work in the food industry my entire life but I would love to work with and around other people. In babysitting Whitley, twice a week, I have learned that I probably do not want to work with children the rest of my life. You see, finding a job in high school can be very beneficial to your career path long term. Thankfully, your job while in high school does not have to be your job forever! However, finding a part time job will enable you to learn to work with bosses and other employees, manage your schedule accordingly, and take up some responsibility of your own. If you are anything like me, you just may meet some of your absolute best friends by making chicken sandwiches.

> ## What are some tips to share with middle schoolers about working as a high school student?
>
> "Make sure to take responsibility and get your school work done to the best of your ability. Do your best at your job. Focus on the task at hand."
>
> **Chloe - High School Junior**

Talk to Your Parents!!

One of the most important conversations you need to have, regarding work, will be the conversation you have with your parents regarding finances and what you will be responsible for while in high school. That conversation took place for me when I began driving on my own. You will soon realize just how much money you can blow through when you start driving. My parents and I decided that I would be responsible for paying for my monthly car insurance and my own gas. The car I am driving now is my dad's old car that I am renting from my parents by paying insurance. At the end of my senior year, I will purchase my own car, with the help of my parents, that I will take to college with me. My little brother will go through the same process as soon as I leave. You see when you begin driving, you are able to just get in the car and go. You are able to get milkshakes with your little brother or go get coffee with a group of friends. If you are anything like me, you will realize that you are going out an insane amount, spending most of your money on food. So, that is just a bit of information for you to keep in the back of your mind when you begin thinking about driving and your use of money.

Every family has their own set of rules when it comes to working. Some families require their children to work in high school. Some families do not care if their children decide to work. I was not required to work. My parents never asked me to get a job or have any type of employment. However, they made clear to me that I would not be given extra cash whenever I wanted to go out. Everything I spent was my own money. My parents told me that if I wanted to go out every night and get dinner with friends that was fine but I would need to find a source of income at some point. Boy, were they right. I was told that there would always be three meals a day available to me at home. I had to start making smart decisions about when I was going to spend my money and when I could have just eaten dinner at home.

I totally understand that every family is different when it comes to working in high school. Whether you have a paid job or not, we are always working. The Lord is always using us to strengthen His kingdom. If you are in a place in your life right now where there is no financial need for you to work, focusing on service could be a great option for you. If working is not a necessity or an option, focus on volunteering at your church to gain experience working with other people. You could even do something so simple as folding the rest of the laundry for your mom before she gets home from work. Service and work can go hand in hand. The difference between service and work is honestly the money side of the job. The money we earn from working is God's money that He has entrusted you with in the first place. And the outcome of our service is all in His hands. It all goes back to Him in the end, and let's be honest, what doesn't?

Proverbs 1:8 says, "Listen, my son, to your father's instruction and do not forsake your mother's teaching." Listen to your parents when they try to share wisdom with you about money and how you should or shouldn't spend it; they know more than you do!! Every time my bank statement comes in the mail, I try to avoid balancing my checkbook at all costs. I absolutely hate doing it. My dad has been so very kind to me and has tried to walk me through the process of balancing every month when a new statement comes in the mail. I can't tell you what it is exactly that I hate so much about the checkbook but my hate for it is real. When I first opened my bank account, I had a lot to learn. I had to learn how to deposit checks, how to write checks, how to withdraw money, and how to balance my checkbook. When my dad tried to teach me about the checkbook, I was pretty standoffish. I did not want to accept help and I did not want to learn an entirely new skill I knew absolutely nothing about.

Like all aspects of your life, your parents are there to help and guide you. I know for me, learning all about finances has been an absolute disaster. I often think about living in the real world by myself and it terrifies me. What if I file my taxes incorrectly? What if I miss a month on paying my rent? Handling money is scary and not always easy for non-math people, like myself. This is why having continual conversations with your parents is so important. This is why accepting help is so critical to you becoming the independent individual you were designed to be. The Lord gave us people, like our parents, to help guide us through these kinds of situations in our lives. Let's not take that for granted, what do you say?

What Do I Do with My Money?

In the world we live in today, money is made out to be the "end-all, be-all." Even though the saying, "Money can't buy happiness," has been around for quite some time we still try to use it for that. I think you and I understand the fact that money cannot make you eternally happy. Money cannot rid you of all the problems you may face in this world. Money is not everything. Proverbs 23:4 says, "Do not wear yourself out to get rich; do not trust your own cleverness." This verse ties together the exact point I am trying to get across when it comes to working in high school. Working for the money is not the only reason working in high school can be beneficial to you in the future. I hate to break it to you but if you are working a part time job, which you probably will be, you won't be making that much to begin with anyway. I believe that in getting your first job in high school, you will be able to gain helpful experience in the workforce that you will carry with you the rest of your life. Trying not to focus all of your attention on the money side of getting a job is definitely difficult. Mark 4:19 tells us, "...but the worries of this life, the deceitfulness of wealth and the desires for other things come in and choke the word, making it unfruitful." There can be danger in wealth, friend; this is why I believe it is so important to answer the question, "What do I do with my money?"

> ## What are some tips to share with middle school girls about work and money management?
>
> "SAVE SAVE SAVE! I got my job and I didn't save a penny of any pay checks until at least 6 months after working. ... You will soon learn what's important - gas money, the lastest shoe, or Starbucks. Don't get me wrong I still get my Starbucks, but I know when is enough and I'm always out for a good deal!"
>
> **Shelby - High School Senior**

Matthew 6:21 says, "For where you treasure is, there your heart will be also." What we do with our money matters, friends. If we spend our money on pop culture magazines, what do you think that says about where our hearts are? If we spend all of our money on new makeup, what do you think that says about where our hearts are? If we spend all of our money on drugs, what do you think that says about where our hearts are? That makes you think, doesn't it? It is hard thinking about things like this. It is hard to evaluate our own hearts and recognize our weaknesses. I totally get that. However, God's word stands. He is very clear in this verse in Matthew.

There was a time in my life that I spent so much money on the expensive Victoria's Secret underwear. Every time I got an email about the 7 for $27 you better believe I was at the mall. I realized something very important about myself once I realized just how much money I was spending on so little clothing. I found a lot of self-validation when it came to the kind of underwear I wore. I didn't want to wear the Target, generic brand underwear. I wanted the tag to say Victoria's Secret. I understand that this may sound super silly to some of you but the truth still stands. I thought that the type of underwear I was wearing made that much of a difference in my everyday life. My heart was totally in the wrong place. I wanted the name brand underwear because it made me feel better about myself knowing I was able to afford fancy underwear that expensive.

Looking back on those days now, I realize how stupid I was. I now love my granny panties from Target and you want to know why? Because I realized that my worth is not found on the name brand tag on my underwear. I loved the fact that I had a job and I was making enough money to purchase that underwear. I Timothy 6:10 says, "For the love of money is a root of all kinds of evil. Some people, eager for money, have wandered from the faith and pierced themselves with many griefs." I believe that taking a long, hard look into your heart is important when talking about money. Do you love money? Is your happiness found in what money can buy you?

The Bible is very clear on the fact that the Lord wishes for us to give. Proverbs 22:9 says, "The generous will themselves be blessed, for they share their food with the poor." Now, I understand that this verse does not specifically say anything about money. However, I believe that the idea of giving your money away is one of the most tangible forms of giving to talk about. Genesis 28:20-22 says, "Then Jacob made a vow, saying, 'If God will be with me and will keep me in this way that I go, and will give me bread to eat and clothing to wear, so that I come again to my father's house in peace, then the Lord shall be my God, and this stone, which I have set up for a pillar, shall be God's house. And of all that you give me I will give a full tenth to you.'" This verse introduces us to the idea of tithing our money. The definition of *tithe* is "the tenth part of agricultural produce or personal income set apart as an offering to God or for works of mercy..." I'm sure if you have grown up in church you have heard this term many times. Tithing is the physical act that we do in order to show our understanding that our money is not ours. Our money, like all things, belongs to the Lord. When we tithe ten percent of our money we are showing how we are willing to give up a portion of our money to the Lord and what He is doing in the world.

There are many other ways in which you can give in addition to tithing. You are capable of giving your time and your energy to another person. You are capable of giving your help or your tangible gifts to another person, as well. The Bible says in 2 Corinthians 9:7, "Each of you should give what you have decided in your heart to give, not reluctantly or under compulsion, for God loves a cheerful giver." I think this is a beautiful picture that I do not want us to miss. The Lord wants us to give. He believes it is important and if we wish to honor Him with our lives, we will most likely find it important as well. I love that fact that Paul says that our giving should not be "under compulsion." If you walked downstairs on Christmas morning and your parents handed you a present and said, "Here you go, daughter. I guess we had to give you something this year," you probably wouldn't find that gift was very special anymore. Right? The same is true with us when it comes to giving. The Lord doesn't want us to give to His kingdom with the attitude of, "I have to." That is just as unappealing to Him as it would be to us. Instead, let's come to Him with a cheerful heart, filled with thanksgiving for the things He has done for us.

MY prayers for YOU: Work it, Girl

To the girl who feels like she has nothing to offer in the workforce, I pray the Lord will show you that you have been blessed with many gifts and abilities. (Ephesians 2:10)

To the girl who is struggling to decide what to do with her money, I pray the Lord will give you clear guidance. (Psalm 32:8)

To the girl who is struggling to give a portion of her money away, I pray the Lord will show you that He will use that to strengthen His kingdom. (Proverbs 3:5-6)

To the girl who is struggling to find a place to serve, I pray the Lord will open doors for you that you did not even know existed. (2 Timothy 2:15)

To the girl who is struggling to accept help from her elders, I pray the Lord will soften your heart and allow you to see just where you need to grow. (James 4:6)

Sweet Whitley Grace (we love selfies!)

*A few of my Chick-fil-A co-workers at our employee
Christmas party!*

3

Boys, Boys, Boys

How Far Is Too Far?

My personal dating experiences have not been very good and not at all what I would have wanted for myself. Starting in about eighth grade actually, I developed a relationship with Jack. I knew that my parents didn't want me dating at the time. The relationship was surrounded by lies and deception because I chose not to tell my parents we were "dating." I was so blinded by his good looks and sweet talk that I completely lost sight of what was important to me: my faith, my family and my friends. The relationship was nothing short of awful. He was never faithful to me and did not respect me whatsoever. He would always be texting and hanging out with other girls telling them the same things he would tell me. The relationship became abusive emotionally, verbally and physically. I felt so trapped. Because of the deception behind our relationship, I was always lying to my parents. I didn't think I could talk to them about what was happening. My relationship with my parents was completely wrecked and there was no trust between us for about five years. I didn't care. I mean I was in love so everything I was doing was okay, right?

The physical line was crossed in many ways with Jack. He was my first everything. I believed I was so in love with him that nothing mattered, not even my boundaries. I gave him everything I had and then some. In the end, it broke my heart and left me feeling ashamed and unwanted in so many ways. When you are in a relationship and it gets physical, it is very hard to stop. My Great-Aunt Sue will always be one of the greatest women I have ever had the privilege to know. She would always say, "You can never go back to just holding hands." She was so right. Once that physical line is crossed, why stop right?

> *Where is the physical line when you are in a dating relationship with someone?*
>
> "I would take things very slow and wait to have sex until I am married."
>
> **Elizabeth - 8th Grader**

Jack and I had an "off and on" relationship for a total of five years. In one of those off periods, I dated Blake, one of my really good friends my freshman year. He pursued my heart well and wanted me to see for so long that I was worth more than I thought. I told my parents about this relationship and they were involved from the beginning. Eventually, I broke up with him because I was so scared. I was terrified by how I was feeling. I was terrified at how different my relationship with him was from anything I had with Jack. There was a large gap in our friendship for a while after we broke up. He continued to love and care for me even after our relationship ended. He is one of my closest friends to this day. I am forever thankful for the way he treated me while we were together.

I tell everyone that because of the lack of physicality I had with Blake, we are able to remain such good friends. I honestly believe that. The more physical you get with your guy, the harder it is to remain friends if you two eventually break up. In all of our bodies there is an autonomic nervous system, or the ANS. A huge function of the ANS revolves around sexual stimulation. Likewise, oxytocin is an incredibly strong chemical in all women's brains (in men's brains it is called vasopressin). Oxytocin washes over our brains any time we are intimate with someone. Author

Dannah Gresh defines oxytocin as "sexual superglue."[1] The Lord gave us oxytocin because it is an addictive substance. The more intimate you become with your boyfriend, the more oxytocin is released, "super-gluing" yourself to him.

Within the context of marriage, oxytocin is a beautiful thing. Proverbs 5:18-19 says, "May your fountain be blessed, and may you rejoice in the wife of your youth, A loving doe, a graceful deer may her breasts satisfy you always, may you ever be captivated by her love." That is what marriage was designed for!! God designed your husband to be captivated by your love and your love only. But in a dating relationship, the more oxytocin your brain releases, because of an intimate situation, the more you are sexually super-gluing yourself to someone who is not your husband.

> ## Where is the physical line when you are in a dating relationship with someone?
>
> "I wish I would have set the line at kissing. Many relationships are too focused on physical aspects and lose the real meaning (behind them)."
>
> **Sloan - High School Sophomore**
>
> "I think the physical line is different for everyone depending on a lot of factors, but I think it is important to remember that once you've gone past a certain point, you can't go back. Even though it's phsyical, emotions are also invovled so I think it's important to establish boundaries in the beginning of youre relationship."
>
> **Heather - High School Senior**

Think about it this way, everything you do with your boyfriend NOW is something that you and your future husband will probably have to have a conversation about LATER. The same goes for your boyfriend and his future wife. You need to decide now where you draw the line and you need to respect that line, no matter how difficult it may seem. I totally understand that being caught up in the moment can seem like a fun and spontaneous experience for you in high school. It may be fun and it may be spontaneous, that is true. However, is it worth the superglue? Is it worth being emotionally and physically connected to someone who is not your husband? It is very uncommon that you will marry your high school boyfriend. (That is important to remember.) These are hard questions you will need to answer before you decide to engage in a dating relationship.

Unfortunately, Jesus doesn't give us girls a "dating guide" telling us how far you should or shouldn't go with your boyfriend. That is the beauty of the Garden of Eden in Genesis. He gave Adam and Eve a choice to obey and respect His boundaries. He gives you and me that same choice. Paul states it so clearly in Ephesians 5:3, "But among you there must not be even a hint of sexual immorality, or of any kind of impurity, or of greed, because these are improper for God's holy people."

As I stated before, you need to decide where you draw the line when it comes to physicality. Here is an example of the chain of events that could occur in a "spur of the moment" situation:

1. Being alone with the opposite sex
2. Holding hands
3. Long hugs
4. Quick kisses
5. Vertical make out session
6. Touching above the waist
7. Horizontal make out session
8. Touching below the waist
9. Taking clothes off
10. Sexual intercourse[2]

Proverbs 4:26-27 says,

> Make level paths for your feet
> and take only ways that are firm.
> Do not swerve to the right or the left;
> keep your foot from evil.

High schools are typically a lot larger than middle schools. There will be a lot of new, cute boys to interact with. Guard your hearts, ladies. You will slip up and fall into some situations you wish you hadn't. I get that. You will meet some Jacks in your life. Some boys will break your heart. Some boys will make you feel like you're on top of the world. Solomon tells us in Proverbs 4:23, "Above all else, guard your heart, for it is the wellspring of life." Jesus gives us one heart and one body. Let's treat them both with respect and save our oxytocin to enjoy with our future husbands!

Keep Your Friends in the Loop!

Do not shut your friends out of your dating relationship. One thing I learned from my relationship with Jack is that if you're hiding it, it is probably wrong. And that is so true. If you are in a relationship with a boy and it is positive and healthy you won't want to hide it. Community is so important when it comes to relationships.

My senior year of high school I received the opportunity to date Matthew. We had been friends for about two years before we started dating. We went to prom together my junior year and he decided around that time he had feelings for me. I was still recovering from my relationship from Jack, and I continued to push Matthew away for about 6 months.

What would be a fun date?

"I am an outdoorsy person, so getting some food & going on a hike is always really fun. Or maybe just driving to a scenic place to chill for a while."

Winnie - High School Junior

One of the things I have learned about dating this year has been that group dates are awesome! Going to get dinner with a group of friends is a great thing. Sure, it isn't a "one on one" date with your guy but come on, those aren't always fun to begin with, right? One of the main things my mom told me that she regrets from her high school dating years was that she shut out so many of her friends just to spend time with her high school sweetheart, who happens to be my dad. When I was dating Jack, everything was hidden. It was like living in darkness to some extent. I felt dirty and lonely. A huge reason I decided not to let people into my relationship with Jack is because I knew the things we were doing were wrong and unhealthy for us both. That is exactly what Adam and Eve did in the Garden of Eden. What did they do when they realized they had messed up? They tried to hide. They tried to hide from each other by covering themselves with fig leaves and they tried to hide from God among the trees, hoping He would not see them.

In dating Matthew, I am able to have open conversations with my friends about what is going on between us, and they offer me feedback. Sometimes my friends and I have fun conversations about our relationship like what our first date was like. However, I know that I am being held accountable by three really solid girls who have my back and with whom I'm growing closer to the Lord. As hard as it was to learn this lesson, I am so glad that I eventually did. Community is one of the most beautiful things the Lord has given us. Let's not overlook it, what do you say?

Now, keeping your friends involved in your relationship doesn't mean kissing your boyfriend every time you two are around a group of your friends. That will get really annoying for everyone very fast. Instead, be together with a group of people. Enjoy the company of your friends and engage with them. Group dates are a time to be with everybody, not just your boyfriend.

> *Do you believe having community involved in your dating relationships is a healthy thing to do?*
>
> "Yes. I dated a guy my sophomore year of high school and thought he was a great guy. But he kept me away from my family and friends which ended up being a really bad situation for me. So talk to your friends and family about your relationship because they can see huge red flags popping up when you can't."
>
> **Anna - High School Senior**

Community is defined as "a group of men or women leading a common life according to a rule." Ecclesiastes is a book of the Old Testament Bible written by Solomon. I mentioned this verse earlier when I referred to "study buddies." However, I noticed that it comes into play again when we are talking about community being involved in our dating relationships.

Two are better than one,
because they have a good
return for their work:
If one falls down,
his friend can help him up.
But pity the man who falls
and has no one to help him up!
(Ecclesiastes 4:9-10)

Solomon paints a brief but powerful picture of community. A phrase as simple as "falls down" can have multiple meanings. If you choose to surround yourself with people who want to pursue the Lord with you, you will always have someone to catch you when you fall. Did you have a crappy day at school? Your friend will be there to help pick up your spirits. Did you go a little too far with your guy when he came over last night? Your girl will be there to pick you up, and confront and challenge you. She may even help you decide what kind of conversation you need to have with your boyfriend to keep it from happening again.

Community is a beautiful thing that the Lord designed. He designed it to be a safe place for us to live together. Enjoy it. Pursue the Lord together. I promise you, there is nothing like it.

"And let us consider how we may spur one another on toward love and good deeds. Let us not give-up meeting together, as some are in the habit of doing, but let us encourage one another..." Hebrews 10:24-25

Redemption

If I could write an entire book on redemption and what that word means to me I would do it. I love it so much I want to have it tattooed on my body! For me this word has come into play specifically when it comes to relationships. When I was dating Jack, I did and said things I never imagined I would. After I broke up with him the summer before my junior year, I felt worthless. I felt like no one would ever want me after all he and I had done, and I was so broken. I believed so many lies in that time, and they destroyed me. "Megan, no one could ever love you. You're dirty, worthless, and unlovable." Those words circulated through my head for so long. The fact of the matter is that those words are simply not true and I had to learn to replace those lies with the Lord's truth. "Megan, you are made new. You are beautiful, loved, valued, and redeemed."

Want to know a secret? That is the truth about who I am AND about who you are!!! Waking up every day striving to believe those truths is a daily struggle. I am still often tempted to believe that I am worth nothing and that I am a lost cause. The Christian artist Matthew West came out with a song recently called Mended. I absolutely love the lyrics and I believe that they really help put into perspective just how incredibly big the Lord's love is for me and for you.

You see your worst mistake
But I see the price I paid
There's nothing you could ever do, to lose what grace has won
So, hold on, it's not the end
No, this is where love's work begins
I'm making all things new
And I will make a miracle of you

When you see broken beyond repair
I see healing beyond belief
When you see too far gone
I see one step away from home
When you see nothing but damaged goods
I see something good in the making
I'm not finished yet
When you see wounded, I see mended

I see my child, my beloved
The new creation you're becoming
You see the scars from when you fell
But I see the stories they will tell
You see worthless, I see priceless
You see pain, but I see a purpose
You see unworthy, undeserving
But I see you through eyes of mercy.[3]

That is who you are. No matter how many mistakes you make you will always be His and you can always return to the One who made you.

You will make mistakes when it comes to relationships. You may say something you wish you hadn't or you may do things with your guy that you will regret later on in your life. I get it. I am right there with you.

Just because we have this promise of forgiveness and redemption does not mean that we can just do whatever we want whenever we want. We, as followers of Christ, have a responsibility to remain pure and holy. Paul says in I Corinthians 6:18, "Flee from sexual immorality. All other sins a man commits are outside his body, but he who sins sexually sins against his own body." This is a commandment from the Lord that we are called to obey. Don't hide yourself in the fig leaves. Live in the freedom and everlasting joy that the Lord has offered you, through His boundaries, because He loves you!!!!

Think about David in the Bible. Acts 13:22 tells us that he was "a man after God's own heart." Do you know what David did? David was an adulterer and a murderer and yet the Lord came to earth through the lineage of David. In Psalm 51 David cries out to the Lord saying...

> Have mercy on me, O God,
> according to your unfailing love;
> according to your great compassion
> blot out my transgressions.
> Wash away all my iniquity
> and cleanse me from my sin.

I know when I was at my darkest I cried out to God just like David did. I said some of the same words. There will be times in your life that you feel like all you can do is cry out to him. I have been there. I get it. Here is some good news for you. Psalm 103 says this,

> Praise the Lord, O my soul
> And forget not all his benefits—
> who forgives all your sins,
> and heals all your diseases,
> who redeems your life from the pit
> and crowns you with love and compassion...

What a love we have in our Jesus. He forgives all our sins. He redeems us from the pit we have gotten ourselves into.

MY prayers for YOU: Boys, Boys, Boys

To the girl who is hurting from past relationships, I pray that you will have the Lord's peace to sustain you today and always. (Colossians 3:15)

To the girl who is lonely and wishing for a relationship, I pray that you will see the Lord as your true love and the pursuer of your heart. (Jeremiah 29:11)

To the girl who is stuck in a relationship she knows she shouldn't be in, I pray you have the strength that only comes from the Lord to end it and to live in His freedom. (Romans 3: 23-25)

To the girl who feels like she has done everything right her whole life and is crippled by anxiety, I pray you will feel His calming spirit and be freed. (Psalm 94:19)

To the girl who feels like she is a lost cause and redemption is too far away for her to even see, I pray you will know that the Lord has redeemed you and your story for His good and perfect plan. (Isaiah 61:3)

4

BeYOUtiful

What Were Our Bodies Created For?

We talked earlier, in chapter three, the dating portion of this book, about the autonomic nervous system found in all human bodies. Remember how we said that the ANS is the system of our bodies that greatly revolves around sexual stimulation? Well, the ANS for girls is a little slower in reacting than the ANS for males. To be blunt, that essentially means that we do not get turned on as quickly as guys do. That gives us girls incredible power and with that power comes a great responsibility. You have probably heard it said that boys fall in love with their eyes. This is true. You know when you wear that low-cut shirt you may get a couple more glances than normal, right? We both know that this is a real thing. The saying "dressing to impress" is a very real thing in today's world. Why do you think that we like wearing those sheer shirts with really tight jeans when we are going out? We have a desire to wear those things because we are aware of our power.

Paul tells us in I Corinthians 6:19-20, "Do you not know that your body is a temple of the Holy Spirit, who is in you, whom you have received from God? You are not your own; you were bought with a price. Therefore, honor God with your body." Let's break down this passage. Verse 19 asks a question. Do you know that your body is a temple for the Holy Spirit to live in? Can you answer this question honestly? I know when I was in middle school I definitely could not. Do you understand how much of an honor that is? Psalm 100:3 says, "Know that the Lord is God. It is he who made us, and we are his; we are his people, the sheep of his pasture." We mean something. Our bodies were created for the Lord to live in us and through us. God created us in His image intentionally for us to bring Him glory. God sent His Son to die for our sins and for us to be "bought with a price." That is an honor and privilege not to be taken lightly. Verse 20 says that because of this truth, we are to honor the Lord with our bodies. We were bought with a price. Jesus' death on the cross allowed us freedom through Him. That is awesome. That is an honor. So, what do we do with these bodies that the Lord has given to us?

We all know how difficult it is to live in a world that has been overtaken by sex. Sexual images are all over the place and we, boys and girls alike, have become desensitized to it. I already talked about how "boys fall in love with their eyes" and how that gives us, as women, extreme power. I Peter 4:10 tells us this, "As each has received a gift, use it to serve one another, as good stewards of God's varied grace." Peter tells us very clearly that we have a responsibility to serve others with our bodies. Now I understand that sounds weird, but let me explain. Because we are women, the world often tells us that we are to use our bodies as objects. And, sadly, many women fall into the trap of accentuating their sexuality and using that power for their own agendas. Our bodies, even as women, were not created for that purpose. Our bodies were created to bring honor to the Lord and to worship Him.

One way you can serve the Lord and the people around you, boys specifically, is by not dressing in a way that would cause them to look. In doing this, we are serving them by helping them with their daily struggle with lust and sinful thoughts. I, personally, used to be very frustrated when my mom first started explaining this to me. I would always say, "it's their fault for looking in the first place!" Talk about selfish, am I right? They do choose to look, yes. But, we also have a responsibility to assist them in that struggle. When you dress in a way that is modest, you are showing that you value another person's spiritual life more than you value your desire to wear clothing you know may not be the best choice.

Another way we can use our bodies for the good of others, specifically other girls, is by asking God to help us in "taming our tongue." James 3:8 says, "but no human being can tame the tongue. It is a restless evil, full of deadly poison." I think you and I both know what James is talking about. Gossip. Gossip is an easy trap to fall into. I fall into it each and every day. I'm sure you do as well. Gossip becomes an even larger issue once you reach high school. Everything seems like it becomes a much bigger deal and because of that, there are more things to talk about. "Did you hear what Sally said about Morgan?" "Did you hear what Jess did at the party last Friday?" "Did you hear about Seth and Alyssa?" I'm sure sentences like these and more will come up at some point during your high school days but, here's the deal, we like gossip. You can say you don't all day long, but you do. We like to gossip because it gives us a sense of belonging. We, especially as women, crave that belonging and want to fit in somewhere.

When we gossip, we feel like we are in "the know." We feel like we are being a part of something. We also gossip in order to make ourselves feel "more-than" or "above" other girls. You and I both know that is true and we do it to boost our self-esteem. However, here is the bad news. Once you start gossiping, it is very hard to stop because it is so easy. Talking is one of the things, as human beings, we do without even thinking half of the time. Once we start talking it is hard to stop especially if you are frustrated with a situation. We have got to pray for God to help us tame our tongues and remember to only speak and think about "whatever is true, whatever is noble, whatever is right, whatever is pure, whatever is lovely, whatever is admirable, excellent or praiseworthy" (Philippians 4:8).

Jesus put on the form of a human body in order to serve. He came to Earth as a man to serve others. He physically endured the worst kind of death in human history in order to serve others. Matthew 20:28 says, "Even the Son of Man came not to be served but to serve, and to give his life as a ransom for many." We, as Christians, have received the gift of grace and forgiveness from the Lord. Because of that gift, we have a responsibility to serve others with our bodies in any way we can. We have a responsibility to "go and make disciples of all nations" (Matthew 28:19). I think about it this way, John 1:14 tells us, "The Word became flesh and made his dwelling among us." In this passage, John is referring to "The Word" as Jesus. The Word came to the earth in bodily form to be with His people. When you think about all Jesus did, as a human being, how could we not want to worship Him? How could we not be willing to serve Him and others any way we can? How could we not fall on our knees and thank Him for everything He has done?

Inner Beauty is the Real Winner

Do something for me really quick. Think of 10 things you love about yourself when you look in the mirror. Got them? Okay, now think of 10 things you do not love about yourself when you look in the mirror. If you are anything like me, you probably came up with a lot more answers for the second option than you did for the first one. I totally get it. Do you feel like you are consumed with the thoughts of what others think about you when you show up to school? Do you feel like you have to look perfect every day at school? Do you feel like you will never look the way you want to look? I have answered "yes" to all of these questions at some point or another in my life. It sucks. It really does.

> *When you look in the mirror, what do you see? What do you wish you saw?*
>
> "I always point out what is wrong with my body. I wish I was skinnier."
>
> **Grace - 8th Grader**

When I was about six years old, my family lived in Colombia, South Carolina. We lived there for five years. A lot of great things came out of our time there like the birth of my sweet baby brother! However, there was one situation that came from our time there that ruined the view I had of myself for a long period of time. I was in first grade and I loved doing gymnastics every week! It brought me so much joy. One day, I went home from school with my friend Michelle. Michelle and I were in the same gymnastics class together. I was so excited to get to go home from school with her and then go to our class together. When it was time to change into our outfits I put on my leotard and headed to the car. I will never forget those few minutes standing in her driveway waiting for her mom to come outside. Michelle took one look at me and said, "Megan you're too fat for your leotard." I vividly remember standing there touching my stomach and losing all confidence in my body.

That was the day when I began to be consumed with thoughts of my body. Gymnastics was never the same for me. I dreaded getting into that pink velvet leotard. I remember one day I told myself, "You know what Megan, you are fat and there is nothing you can do about it so you better just accept it." I told myself every day that I was fat as a defense mechanism. I remember one day I was in the shower and I scratched my stomach so many times that there were red marks all over my torso. I was only 10 years old. I told myself that everyone already thought I was fat so whenever I was in conversations with people I would make comments like, "I'm fat, I know." I would then laugh it off like it was no big deal. In doing this, I believed that I was preventing myself from ever hearing those words from anyone ever again. Little did I know that I was continually distorting the thoughts in my head and, ultimately, attacking my heart. I was literally waking up every morning with the mindset that I was never going to be good enough in a physical sense. I was never diagnosed with an eating disorder. However, looking back on my years in middle school I probably could have been. There were times I would try to make myself throw up but I never succeeded. I had a disease that developed from believing lies about myself. That is not a fun sickness to suffer from.

> *If you could leave a note of encouragement to a middle school girl about body image, what would you say?*
>
> "Looks will not be there when we are older. It's what's on the inside that counts and will last forever!"
>
> **Loftyn - High School Sophomore**

I tell you this story not to make you feel bad for me. I made a decision to tell myself those things for as long as I did. I share this story with you in order to show you that the things I was telling myself were simply not true. If you notice that you are beginning to say similar things to yourself as I did, I am here to tell you that what you are saying to yourself is NOT TRUE. Here is the heart of what I am trying to say: your outer beauty will fade. You will eventually lose those curves and your skin will not always be acne free. Like all things of this world, physical beauty does not last. We should redefine beauty the way that God's word does. I Peter 3: 4 says, "Instead, it should be that of your inner self, the unfading beauty of a gentle and quiet spirit which is of great worth in God's sight." Your inner beauty is what will remain constant all the way to eternity.

Have you have ever compared yourself to someone else? Have you have ever felt jealous of another girl's appearance? Have you have ever worried about what others think you look like? I know I have! I Samuel 16:7 says, "But the Lord said to Samuel, 'Do not consider his appearance or his height, for I have rejected him. The Lord does not look at the things man looks at. Man looks at the outward appearance, but the Lord looks at the heart.'" Phew. How about that? That is pretty straightforward if you ask me. Ladies, even if we use our new definition of beauty, believing you are beautiful is hard. I for one know how hard it is! The devil is evil and he will use anything he can to make you feel horrible about yourself. He's done it to me and he will do it to you if you're not careful. So how do we do we fight him? How do we get to a place where we feel like we are valued, loved and truly beautiful? I believe that it starts with accepting who you are and praising the Lord for the way he created you! Psalm 139:14 says, "I praise you because I am fearfully and wonderfully made; your works are wonderful, I know that full well." This is truth ladies! You are fearfully and wonderfully made by a God who sent his Son to die for you! You are beautiful and you are loved. I know that these truths are hard to accept during your everyday lives. If you wake up every morning and CHOOSE to believe that you are beyond beautiful, and wonderfully made by the Creator of the universe, because He is inside your heart, it will dramatically change the way you ever thought you could view yourself. Trust me.

The Culture is Crap

Our culture in this day and age is something else isn't it, ladies? Pictures of women are posted all over the place on billboards and magazine covers strictly to exploit their sexuality in order to sell something. It seems like all it takes is a little nudity and you're all set for the pop culture world. This past fall I started watching The Bachelor. My best friend, Kaytlin, and

I watched the premier episode because we needed a good laugh that particular day. However, I found myself instantly hooked. I just had to see who Nick decided to keep on the show and who he ultimately ended up asking to marry him! I was watching The Bachelor every Monday night, and every Monday night, I found myself angry. I noticed a recurring pattern with the women on the show. Their clothing became more and more scandalous; their actions became more and more promiscuous. I asked myself, "Why"? Why did these women feel that the only way to get Nick's attention was to take their clothes off? Why did these women feel that the only way to stay on the show was to prove their sexuality to him in some way?

The most hated candidate for Nick's hand, twenty-four-year-old Corinne, answered my questions. In one of the very first episodes, Corinne tries to seduce Nick in order to keep their "sexual connection alive." She says that she has a surprise planned for him that will, "make him excited and wanting more." She also says that the surprise will, "keep him thinking about me after." She then proceeds to seduce him by hardly wearing any clothing and by acting "sexy." The whole situation was very sexual and uncomfortable for the other women in the house and the viewer. When asked about the situation Corinne says, "I know what men like and I'm willing to do whatever it takes to get Nick."

> *When you look in the mirror what do you see? What do you wish you saw?*
>
> All I see is fat. I wish I was a better-looking Megan.
> **Megan - 7th Grader**

Some women may commend Corinne for her determination to go after what she wanted. I, however, find what she did that night to be quite saddening. Corinne suffers from something that is common for most women. We all want to be desired. We all want to be wanted. Men struggle with this as well, but it expresses itself in different ways. As women, we sometimes use our bodies to get physical attention from men in order to fill the void we feel in our hearts. There is an old saying my mom once told me, "Women use sex to get love and men use love to get sex." Women use their sexuality in order to feel loved and accepted. Men use their words to make women fall in love with them in order to get sex in return. The sad thing about this truth is that the world encourages us to do this. The world throws sexual images and thoughts our way at every turn. You have seen it and so have I. Our culture has not only distorted our view of what the "perfect body" is supposed to look like but it is also trying to tell us how the "perfect woman" is supposed to act.

The fact of the matter is, ladies, there is no perfect body. Not a single one of us can have a perfect body because the standard of "perfect" changes all the time. Let's travel back and see what the "perfect body" looked like about 100 years ago in America. Beginning in the 1900's the slender, tall, and large bust look was all the rage. Women at this time were seen as healthy and often physically active. Then came the roaring 20's and the age of the Flappers. During the twenties, women and men alike were seen as immature and crazy, if you will. Women at the time began to dress more scandalously, revealing their ankles, knees and legs with the dresses they wore. They were not considered to be super thin but they did have more boyish figures with their desire for a straight torsos and short hair. The 30's and 40's resulted in The Great Depression and wartime. During the war, attractive women had a broad shoulder width and were considered curvier and less skinny. The 50's brought the age of big busts and the hourglass figure. Makeup also became important to women at the time and they soon began to desire the flawless skin look.

When do you feel the most beautiful?

"I feel the most beautiful before school dances when my friends do my hair and makeup and I wear a pretty dress."

Sonia - High School Sophomore

"When my makeup is on fleek and I'm wearing a cute outfit!"

Caroline - 7th Grader

You may have heard of the famous model "Twiggy." Her name explains the body type of the 60's. Twiggy weighed in at 112 pounds and promoted the image of a super skinny body with little breasts and a little butt. The age of Twiggy carried on into the 70's with the increase of Anorexia Nervosa and the introduction of dieting pills. The 80's brought the age of supermodels and fitness. Women desired a toned, slender body. The 90's brought back skinny with the "Heroin Chic" desired look. Women began to idolize the super skinny, almost boney, look.[1] Unfortunately, this look is still a part of our culture today. You want to know something crazy? A plus size model, ten years ago, wore a size 12-18 in pants. Today, plus size models range from a size 6-14 in pants. Jennifer Lawrence, lead actress in the marvelous Hunger Games series, says in an interview with Entertainment Weekly, "I'm never going to starve myself for a part. I don't want little girls to be like, 'Oh, I want to look like Katniss, so I'm going to skip dinner!' [...]I was trying to get my body to look fit and strong, not thin and underfed." What a gal. Jennifer has been rumored to be a size 6. A size 6 is considered a plus sized woman and that is not at all what I think of when I see Jennifer Lawrence. Jennifer, you know what's up.

My favorite book of all time is Redeeming Love by Francine Rivers. Redeeming Love is a hard read, and the story is unimaginable. It captivates me every time. I read it once a year and I still can't get enough. Angel, the main character, is sold into prostitution at a very young age and has lived a life of shame, fear, and guilt. Michael is a devout Christian trusting the Lord while seeking a wife. The analogy of Angel and Michael's relationship is a picture of our relationship with the Lord. The story is so captivating because it is your story and my story. We are Angel. We are shameful human beings who never feel like we will ever be enough. We feel we are undeserving of such a love. Michael is Jesus. His everlasting pursuit of our hearts is unimaginable. One of my favorite lines in this novel comes from a dialogue between Michael and Angel. "Angel looked up at him and saw the sheen of moisture in his eyes. Shock ran through her. "Are you crying? For me?" she said weakly. "Don't you think you're worth it?" (Michael replies).[2] The Lord cries for you every time you look in the mirror and feel that you are not beautiful enough or good enough by the world's standards. I have cried tears of anger and frustration because of my body. All the while I was crying those tears, the Lord was crying for me to believe the truth about who I am. He was crying for me to see that I am fearfully and wonderfully made. He cries those same tears for you, ladies. You are beautiful. You are fearfully and wonderfully made.

You were thought of at the beginning of creation by the Creator of the universe (Jeremiah 1:5). I don't care what the world says. Do you think you're worth it? Jesus does.

"It's two in the morning and I'm still awake in my bed
And I can't shake these lies that keep running around in my head
What if I saw me the way that you see me
What if I believed it was true
What if I traded this shame and self-hatred
For a chance at believing you
That you knit me together in my mother's womb
And you say that I've never been hidden from you
And you say that I'm wonderfully, wonderfully made
You search me and know me
You know when I sit, when I rise
So you must know the choices I've made and the pain that I hide..."[3]
-Ellie Holcomb

To the girl who looks in the mirror and hates what she sees, I pray you will see yourself through the Lord's eyes. (Psalm 139:14)

To the girl who feels like she will never be good enough, I pray you will know that the Lord thought you were good enough to die for. (I John 3:1)

To the girl who is slowly dying because of what she is doing to her own body, I pray you will have the strength of the Lord to rejuvenate your body to its full potential. (Philippians 4:13)

To the girl who physically hurts her own body to distract herself from the emotional hurt going on inside her, I pray the Lord will give you peace and strength to deal with the things you are feeling. (Colossians 1:13)

To the girl who edits everything out of her own pictures because she cannot bear to make public what she views as her flaws, I pray you will understand that when Jesus sees you, He views you as flawless. (Isaiah 1:18)

5

Fam Jam

Broken Lives Make Broken Families

The definition of *family* is "a basic social unit consisting of parents and their children, considered as a group, whether dwelling together or not." All of that sounds fine and dandy until you reach the last part of that definition. I find the ending quite saddening. "Whether dwelling together or not." I feel like the word "family" can have a positive or negative connotation depending on the person. When I hear the word I automatically think of my two parents, Heather and David. I have been absolutely blessed with the immediate family the Lord gave me. However, I am not naive to the fact that this is not the case for everyone. I am well aware that the world we live in is a broken and sinful place and because of that, nothing is the way it was intended to be in the beginning; this includes families. Families are broken in different ways. I see divorce every day. I see broken sibling relationships among my friends every day. I see brokenness between my peers and their parents every day. Romans 3:23 says very clearly, "For all have sinned and fall short of the glory of God." Every single human who has ever walked this earth has sinned and because of that, nothing is the way it was created to be.

The very first family to ever be on the earth was as broken as can be. Genesis 3:6 says, "When the woman saw the fruit of the tree was good for food and pleasing to the eye, and also desirable for gaining wisdom, she took some and ate it. She also gave some to her husband, who was with her and he ate it." We could spend hours talking about the theological aspects behind this passage but, for our purposes, we will look at it in a very general light. The first two married people were sinful human beings and chose to go their own way when it came to living life with the Lord. Think about Adam and Eve's sons, Cain and Abel. Genesis 4:8 says, "Now Cain said to his brother Abel, 'Let's go out to the field.' While they were in the field, Cain attacked his brother Abel and killed him." This is heavy stuff we are talking about, ladies. I am not telling you these things to scare you or to make you uncomfortable. I tell you these things because I have talked to many girls your age who are afraid of opening up about their family lives because of how broken it is. Here's the deal: you are not alone.

> ## What are some things you wish you could change about your family?
>
> "I wish that they were more sensitive to my brother and I wish that my dad would want to do stuff with me and my sister ..."
> **Adaline - 8th Grader**

I met one of my very best friends to this day about two years ago. Hailey Chapman (also known as the cover artist of this book) has shared with me the brokenness within her own family. She has shared with me the heartbreak of being the oldest child living among divorced parents, who are both remarried. In her own words, "Everything that's going on with my family just really shows why God never intended for people to divorce, you know? It literally affects every single part of my life and my whole family's lives even though the (initial) divorce happened a long time ago." Hailey has struggled with making her family's past mistakes her identity. She has told me she struggles with believing that her family's mistakes have put a "mark" of sorts on her and her future. Watching Hailey care for her 8 siblings (half, step, and real) has been amazing. I am so thankful

I have gotten to walk with her through life the past two years. She has been so kind and so gracious to them. Her younger brother, closest to her, and their younger half-sister have struggled throughout high school to stay away from things that they both know are wrong. Watching Hailey care for them and pursue them with the Lord's love has been so incredible and so sweet for me to witness.

I understand that many girls have been wounded by one or both of their parents in the line of fire of divorce. One of my good friends when I was in elementary school was living through her parents' divorce and it was all happening because her father chose to walk out on their family. She was angry. She was hurt. She was confused. But broken families can also happen for many reasons other than divorce. One of my closest guy friends, Daniel, has struggled with dealing with his father's alcohol addiction. His father chose alcohol over Daniel many times. The hurt that he had caused their family was so difficult for me to watch Daniel go through. Ephesians 4:32 says, "Be kind and compassionate to one another, forgiving each other, just as in Christ God forgave you." This topic is hard to talk about because of the amount of hurt that can come from father/daughter, father/son or mother/daughter, mother/son relationships. There is a lot of it, friends, I know you know that.

The fact of the matter is, because of the brokenness that encompasses our world, our families are broken and our families always will be. My parents have been married for 24 years. They were high school sweethearts and they show their love for each other, to my brother, and to me every day. On the outside, it may seem like we have it all together. Heather and David Bokowy will be the first people to inform you that we most certainly do not have it all together. We still struggle. We still argue. We still worry. Just because my parents are still married does not mean that we are perfect and just because other people's parents are not still married does not mean that they are permanently damaged. Please hear me say this! Your family's past does not need to be your future. The Lord did amazing things through Adam and Eve's broken and sinful family. I have faith He will do the same with yours as well.

Siblings and Parents and Boundaries, Oh My!

You have read a little previously on my relationship with Jack. When I dated Jack, I knew it was wrong. I knew my parents were not okay with me dating at the time. I knew that by being with Jack, I was breaking my family's rule. I chose to isolate myself from my family for about five heartbreaking years. I told myself that I should no longer be a part of my family because of the lack of respect I had shown them and the number of rules I had broken. Looking back on the years I wasted on myself and my own selfishness, I noticed one thing that I hope I will never lose sight of moving forward. It is the greatest "B" word there is: Boundaries. Parents who set boundaries for you are not setting them because they want to be a buzzkill to all of your fun. They set boundaries because that is what the Lord has commanded them to do and because they love you!! Proverbs 22:6 says, "Train up a child in the way he should go; even when he is old he will not depart from it." Think back to the Garden of Eden. God gave Adam and Eve a boundary, "You are free to eat from any tree in the garden; but you must not eat from the tree of the knowledge of good and evil..." (Genesis 2:16-17) I'm sure you already know the story so I will try to not bore you too badly. Adam and Eve disregarded the boundary the Lord gave them and in the end, changed the course of mankind forever. Because they did not trust that the Lord had their best interest at heart, they chose to go their own way and ended up hurting themselves more than they could ever have imagined.

When your parents tell you to be home by 10 or 11pm it is not because they do not want you to have any fun with your friends in high school. I understand how you could feel that way about them and their rules. I used to feel that way about my parents and their family rules for a very long time! The fact of the matter is, boundaries are good. We were intended to live within the boundaries set for us by the authority placed above us. The Lord gave us the Ten Commandments as boundaries in which to live our lives. When we choose to live life within the boundaries set for us, we will live life full of adventure, believe it or not. When we choose to look at boundaries as an act of love, instead of annoying or overbearing, it changes everything.

I said before, I shut my family out of my life for a very long time, keeping my thoughts and actions to myself. This included my relationship with my brother. Ryan Bokowy is the sweetest human being you will ever run into in your lifetime. He is so full of joy and adventure. We are three and a half years apart and for a very long time we did not get along. I fell into the "older child trap" of believing that my parents loved the younger child more than they loved me. I resented him for that, even though it was not true. I also resented him during the time I shut my parents out of my life because I knew that he wasn't breaking nearly as many rules as I was on a daily basis. When I take time to reflect on those years of my life, I discover that I wanted to be just like Ryan and that is why I kept my distance from him for so long.

> ## What are some things you love about your family?
>
> "I love our quirkiness, funny spirits, and semi-enjoyment of learning!"
> **Charlotte - 8th Grader**

My senior year of high school was Ryan's freshman year. He had gone back and forth on whether or not he wanted to go to the same high school I went to, or to go to the local public high school in our town. He chose correctly and came to my school with me! The summer before we began school together we formed a bond like no other. We did just about everything together and it was absolutely awesome. My best friend, Kaytlin, has a younger brother Ryan's age and the four of us made sibling dates our thing! Ryan and I became the best of friends over the summer before his freshman year. I drag him everywhere with me! He tucks me into bed almost every night and we talk about everything. He decided (with a little push from me) to run for freshman class president. He won and instantly became a part of our school's student government family! Having Ryan as a part of my friend group and my life has been the best blessing.

Proverbs 17:17 says, "A friend loves at all times, and a brother is born for a time of adversity." Adversity means, adverse or unfavorable fortune or fate; a condition marked by misfortune or distress." When you look at that verse, then look at the definition of adversity, we see a pretty cool correlation. What would happen if you chose to look at your siblings as your friends?

What would happen if you chose to look at your siblings as a shoulder to cry on instead of a waste of space at your dinner table? The fact of the matter is that the Lord gave us our siblings, just like he has given us everything else. How cool is that? He essentially gave you a friend born straight into your family. Your family would dramatically change if you chose to look at your siblings in that light. I promise.

There are two attributes I have found to be beneficial when it comes to sibling relationships: kindness and forgiveness. Ephesians 4:32 says, "Be kind to one another, tenderhearted, forgiving one another, as God in Christ forgave you." Thank you, Paul, for confirming what I just said! Ryan did not have to forgive me for the pain I had caused our family, but he did. I don't have to choose to be kind to Ryan when he turns into a typical little brother and annoys me at times, but I do. Ask the Lord to redeem your relationship with your sibling. My relationship with Ryan has been totally restored over the past year and he is my absolute best friend. Give it a try. Go find your sibling right now and give them a big hug. You might find that they may need you just as much as you need them.

> *If you could leave a note of encouragement to a middle school girl about family and its impact on your life through high school what would it be?*
>
> "I would say that it is important to spend time with your family and to love them and be kind to them even when you don't get along. I would also say to try your best to get along with your parents because they love you and want the best for you."
>
> **Heather - High School Senior**

Sibling relationships are a hard thing. More times than not, jealousy and pride take over those relationships and send them spiraling down. Relationships between parents and children become so difficult when rules and boundaries are thrown into play. Proverbs 3:5 says, "Trust in the Lord with all your heart, and do not lean on your own understanding." If we truly trust in the Lord's plan for our life, we will have a completely different mindset. We will choose to believe that our parents give us boundaries to abide by because they love us, not because they want to ruin all of our fun. We will choose to believe that the Lord has given us a forever friend in our siblings! The Lord has given us these relationships because, I believe, He wants to use them for great things.

Family x2

I have some great news for you. You and I have both been blessed with two families. You have your earthly family: your biological father, mother, and siblings. You also have been blessed with a spiritual family: your brothers and sisters in Christ. Matthew 12:49-50 says, "Pointing to his disciples, he said, 'Here are my mother and my brothers. For whoever does the will of my Father in heaven is my brother and sister and mother.'" Our earthly family can very well go hand in hand with our spiritual family. My parents and my brother love Jesus with their whole hearts so I have no doubt in my mind that we are a part of the Lord's family as well as our own. That is a very special thing to have. However, I understand that that is not the case for every family. I have plenty of friends who choose to go to church on Sunday morning knowing that their family will not come with them. I understand that sometimes one family member's decision to follow Christ can create a wedge in their relationship with the rest of the family. As sad as that is for me to talk about, I do not want to overlook that fact.

Ephesians 2:19 says, "Consequently, you are no longer foreigners and strangers, but fellow citizens with God's people and also members of his household..." I don't know about you but God's household sounds like the place I want to be, and we get that opportunity! One of the greatest stories in the Bible is the parable of the prodigal son, found in Luke 15:11-32. It goes like this:

"11Jesus continued: "There was a man who had two sons. 12The younger one said to his father, 'Father, give me my share of the estate. So, he divided his property between them.

13"Not long after that, the younger son got together all he had, set off for a distant country and there squandered his wealth in wild living. [14]After he had spent everything, there was a severe famine in that whole country, and he began to be in need. [15]So he went and hired himself out to a citizen of that country, who sent him to his fields to feed pigs. [16]He longed to fill his stomach with the pods that the pigs were eating, but no one gave him anything.

[17]"When he came to his senses, he said, 'How many of my father's hired servants have food to spare, and here I am starving to death! [18]I will set out and go back to my father and say to him: Father, I have sinned against heaven and against you. [19]I am no longer worthy to be called your son; make me like one of your hired servants.' [20]So he got up and went to his father.

"But while he was still a long way off, his father saw him and was filled with compassion for him; he ran to his son, threw his arms around him and kissed him.

[21]"The son said to him, 'Father, I have sinned against heaven and against you. I am no longer worthy to be called your son.'

[22]"But the father said to his servants, 'Quick! Bring the best robe and put it on him. Put a ring on his finger and sandals on his feet. [23]Bring the fattened calf and kill it. Let's have a feast and celebrate. [24]For this son of mine was dead and is alive again; he was lost and is found.' So they began to celebrate."

I copied this story straight from the Bible because there are so many details I do not want us to overlook. There are three specific things I want to point out that this story contains. The first is the fact that this son completely disrespected his father and decided to do life his own way. Essentially what this son is saying to his father by asking for his share of the estate is, "Dad I wish you were dead. Go ahead and give me the money I am entitled to." I know this sounds so harsh but the brutal reality is that we do this each and every day to our Heavenly Father.

The second thing I want to point out is in verses 17 and 18. "When he came to his senses, he said, 'How many of my father's hired servants have food to spare, and here I am starving to death! I will set out and go back to my father and say to him: Father, I have sinned against heaven and against you.'" The son realizes he is in desperate need. He realizes that he needs to change something and he needs to return to his father. I imagine, as this son is walking home, he is rehearsing what he is going to say to his father over and over in his head. He is probably walking with his shoulders and his head down, filled with shame. He is probably expecting the absolute worst to happen when he gets there. I know I have done that plenty of times. I have walked to my parents' room with my shoulders and my head down filled with shame playing my apology to them over and over in my head when I know I have messed up.

> *Have you found that your family in Christ has made an impact on your high school years?*
>
> "Of course! Having a family in Christ makes you feel so encouraged all the time and keeps you going."
>
> **Hyacinth - High School Senior**

The third and final thing I want to point out in this story is found in verse 20. "So he got up and went to his father. But while he was still a long way off, his father saw him and was filled with compassion for him; he ran to his son, threw his arms around him and kissed him." The words that catch my eye are, "But while he was still a long way off…" Do you understand what this means and the beautiful picture that is painted here? This means that the father was eagerly looking for his son to return! He was standing on his porch hoping and praying he would see his son coming home to him. I imagine the father did this every single day after the son left home. The father didn't do this in order to scold his son whenever he came home. He didn't sit on his porch looking for his son to come home so he could yell at him and shame him for leaving. No. He was "filled with compassion for him…" There was no scolding. There was no shaming. There was pure joy and celebration.

"For this son of mine was dead and is alive again; he was lost and is found."

This story is one of pride and abandonment, but also one of redemption and forgiveness. I love this story because I can see myself in the prodigal son when I take a look into my past, and there is a reason for that. This is the picture I want you to see. The father in this story represents our Heavenly Father. Can you take a guess as to who the prodigal son represents? Yes, he represents us. Every single day we say, "Jesus thanks but no thanks. I can do life my own way." Every day we do this and every day we find ourselves in a need to return home. This is also the kind of spiritual family you have. The kind of family that celebrates when you return to the Father. When the Father brings the best robe out for you to wear, puts sandals on your feet and a ring on your finger, and kills the fattened calf for you, your spiritual family drops everything that they are doing to welcome you home and joins the joyous celebration.

We have an awesome privilege to be a part of something so much bigger than ourselves. We become a part of Christ's family when we accept Him as our Father and as our Lord and Savior. John 1:12 says, "Yet to all who did receive him, to those who believed in his name, he gave the right to become children of God." We are his children! He is our perfect Father who loves us with a love that is not possible for us to wrap our minds around. We have been adopted into the family of the Lord and through Him, we have a forever family. Galatians 4:5-7 "To redeem those who were under the law, so that we might receive adoption as sons...So you are no longer a slave, but a son, and if a son, then an heir through God." The family you have in Christ is one you will have the privilege to live with forever. How cool is that?? I can't wait to party with you in Heaven, sweet sister!

MY prayers for YOU: FAM JAM

To the girl who is healing from past wounds inflicted by her family, I pray The Lord will give you comfort knowing He is always with you. (Isaiah 41:10)

To the girl who is struggling to forgive the family who hurt her, I pray the Lord will give you the heart to forgive. (Ephesians 4:32)

To the girl struggling against making her family's past her future, I pray the Lord will show you that your identity is found in Him and Him alone. (Galatians 2:20)

To the girl who struggles to love her siblings, I pray the Lord will soften your attitude towards them and give you the heart to love them. (John 13:34)

To the girl struggling to find a community in which to connect with her family in Christ, I pray the Lord puts people in your life that will show you that community. (Hebrews 10:24-25)

Ryan Bokowy - best brother and best friend all in one human.

Heather and David Bokowy - the greatest people ever.

These are a few of my girlfriends from the month I spent at Malibu. Ecstatic by the fact that I get to spend forever in Heaven with Jesus and their sweet souls!

6

Meg's Declassified Social Survival Guide

Forever Friends

Friendships are one of the Lord's greatest creations. He created community in which we can live life through friendships. He created Eve to be Adam's partner and friend. Jesus knew we couldn't do life alone from the start of creation.

Friendships have been a struggle for me through the course of my middle and high school experience. I attended a small private school from second grade to sixth. The attitude of my grade at that school was very exclusive and not very inviting. The people gave off the idea that you can only have one best friend and that is your best friend forever. You can have other friends but only one BEST friend. That idea is one I took with me for a long time. I tried so hard to find that one friend. However, it never worked out and I found myself very lonely in elementary school leading into middle school. I didn't have that one friend, I had multiple "best friends" and they all ended in conflict. Michelle broke my heart and tainted my view of myself when she called me fat at six years old. Laurel told me in third grade she would rather have Caroline as her best friend. Sara and I went to different high schools and lost touch. Elizabeth decided to date my boyfriend behind my back while they both lied to me about it freshman year. Brooke decided I wasn't good enough for her because I didn't want to party every weekend. I say all that not to scare you or discourage you. Because, trust me, there is hope. Kaytlin Cook is the greatest thing that has ever happened to me. She is the most loyal and incredible friend I have ever had. We have been through so much together and I know we will continue to be friends in the future. You want to know a secret? All of the different friendships I mentioned before were missing something. All of those friendships were rooted in things of the world. Not a single one of those friendships was rooted in our relationships with the Lord.

The book of Job in the Old Testament is one of trial and suffering. Job suffered a great deal in the name of the Lord. But he did have friends that helped him through it all. Job 2:1-13 are all verses dedicated to explaining Job's friends:

> When Job's three friends, Eliphaz the Temanite, Bildad the Shuhite, and Sophar the Naamathite, heard about all the troubles that had come upon him, they set out from their homes and met together by agreement to go and sympathize with him and comfort him.... They sat on the ground with him for seven days and seven nights. No one said a word to him, because they saw how great his suffering was.

Phew. Talk about friendship! Eliphaz was a Temanite, Bildad was a Shuhite and Sophar was a Naamathite. All of these names sound crazy and old fashioned, I know. Naamathites were a tribe of the Gentile race. The Shuhite's origin is unknown and the Temanites were a branch of the Palestinian people. All this to say, the three of these men were from different cultures and different backgrounds than their friend Job. They probably all grew up with their own sets of traditions and rituals, similarly like we do today. What was the one thing all four of these men had in common? It clearly was not their backgrounds. It was their relationship with the Lord. Because of each of their deep-rooted, personal, relationships with the Lord they were able to hold this friendship and be there for Job in a unique way. They were able to sit with him and just be present with him in his time of need. How many of your friends that you have now would be comfortable if you asked them to do that for you? I know I did not have many of those kinds of friends in middle school.

Through Kaytlin, I have been able to learn that having just one "best friend" is no way to live. There will be people throughout your life that you pour into, and people that pour into you. Having both kinds of people in your life is the way to go. Just remember, you cannot pour into others' lives unless you are having your own life poured into as well. Paul writes to the people in Colosse in the book of Colossians in the New Testament. In Colossians 3:13-14 he says, "Bear with each other and forgive whatever grievances you may have against one another. Forgive as the Lord forgave you. And over all these virtues put on love which binds them all together in perfect unity." Let's break this down. Paul uses the terms, "Bear with each other" and, "perfect unity." The definition of the word *bear* is "to hold up; support," and the definition of the word *unity* is "the state of being one; oneness; a whole or totality as combining all its parts into one." Those two words sound like some pretty awesome qualities for a friend to have, right? A good friend is someone you can tell all your secrets to. A great friend is someone who supports you and is one with you in mind and in spirit because of the way the Lord has brought you two together.

> ## How open and honest are you with your friends?
>
> "Very! Your friends know you the best, sometimes better than you know yourself, so let them know what's going on. Friends give the best advice and venting always benefits you both."
>
> **Lenora - High School Senior**

I honestly believe that a friendship, rooted in the Lord, is one that will withstand the hardships and trials this world may send your way. Friendships rooted in things of this world will not last. James writes in James 4:4, "You adulterous people, don't you know that friendship with the world is hatred toward God? Anyone who chooses to be a friend of the world becomes an enemy of God." James says very clearly that when you become "friends" with the things that this world has to offer, you become an enemy of the Lord. Let's be honest, we can all think of some things this world has to offer that may not be the best things for us to fill our lives with: Alcohol being one, drugs being another. Sex and bad relationships may be a third. Those are the easy, tangible ones.

How about the harder, maybe even unseen ones: pride, fear of failure, jealousy, and gossip. These things are still sin, even if they may not be as visible as the previously mentioned ones. I know that I have personally struggled with thinking that my sins were "worse" than other people's just because you could see mine and you couldn't always see theirs.

Friendships are a good thing that the Lord created! One of my favorite stories in the Bible is the story of the Jesus healing the paralytic in Mark chapter 2. This story is one of true friendship. Verse 4 explains the extent these men went to in order to get their friend to Jesus: "Since they could not get him to Jesus because of the crowd, they made an opening in the roof above Jesus and, after digging through it, lowered the mat the paralyzed man was lying on." These men literally carried their friend to the feet of Jesus. Mark tells us that there were four friends who were responsible for carrying their paralyzed friend. Let's talk about the culture at this time. A paralytic was considered an outcast of society. Because they were unable to do anything, they were considered worthless. Paralytics were more than likely living on the streets of the city just desperately hoping for someone who would take care of them. Now clearly, this particular paralytic had some great friends.

Mark is not entirely clear on the details of the previous relationship of the men prior to this day. I believe they were probably friends all along. I believe that they were buddies even before their friend was paralyzed. Think about the conversations these four men must have had leading up to this day. I bet they all loved adventure and all had a sense of great wonder. Because they were carrying their friend, I suspect the trip to Jesus seemed a lot longer than it actually was. One beautiful detail about this story is the fact that even though they could not get their friend to Jesus through the door, they did not give up. They very easily could have just said, "We are too late. Maybe we should try again later." No. They decided to continue the adventure and climb to the roof. They didn't know if they would get in trouble. They didn't know if their plan would even work. Their commitment to get their friend to Jesus is probably one of the greatest qualities these men possessed.

I love this story for many reasons but two in particular. I love the way these four men were so committed to their friend. I also love thinking about how, in order for this plan to work, these four friends had to all be on the same page. They were all headed in the same direction and all had the same mindset. They all had to be 100% okay with the risks and the task in which they were about to embark. If one of the men had backed out the whole story could have ended differently. It took all four of the men, all committed to their friend and to Jesus, to complete this adventure. That sound like some pretty awesome friends to have, don't you think?

Is it Worth It?

For me personally, I have never struggled with a "party longing," if you will. Drinking has never been my thing and I chose to spend my time elsewhere. I totally understand that the party scene is huge in high schools throughout the country. I get it. I think eventually you will have to decide what you think is most important to you.

> *What can you imagine would be a challenging social situation in high school for you and why?*
>
> "Peer pressure because you really want to fit in ..."
> Carter - 8th Grader

In May of 2015, a local middle school in my town went through one of the most traumatic events our city has seen in a long time. Four eighth grade girls were arrested on the charge of possession of child pornography. Allegedly, they witnessed their 13-year old friend being sexually assaulted by their 14-year old guy friend. The guy friend had decided to throw together a little party because his parents were out of town and authorities say that alcohol was definitely involved. The four girls recorded the sexual assault and began sharing the recording via FaceTime. According to an article produced by Fox News, "She [the victim] was found lying naked on the bed in a pool of her own vomit. The victim was reportedly unable to stand on her own and was taken to the hospital."

You may be reading this story thinking to yourself how sick of a world we live in. You are right. However, hear me, the girls and boys in this story are close to our age! Hypothetically speaking, this could happen at your school. The hard truth of the matter is after middle school you begin to gain more and more freedom. You are able to drive to your friends' houses by yourself. You are able to start making your own decisions about with whom you want to hang out with and what you wish to do with you time. I pray you are careful when making these kinds of decisions.

Parties can be a really great thing, and they can still be fun, if executed in a safe manner. For example, after my junior prom, we hosted our after-prom party at my house. That night was one of the greatest nights of my life. Want to know what the best part of the whole night was? Not a single person was drunk. Not a single person was high. We were able to eat good food, play crazy games, hang out by the bonfire my Dad built, play basketball, and just enjoy each other until 6 in the morning. There were about 25 of us who all got together. As mentioned previously, my Dad is the area director for Young Life where I live. He and my Mom sure do know how to have fun without alcohol. I have had multiple friends come up to me this fall and confirm that we are having after-prom at my house again this year!

I actually ended up going to another school's prom a few weeks later. They had their after-prom at an arcade/amusement park. Later on that night, a bunch of people went to one of the football player's house for an "after-after-prom party." He was a senior and was offered a full ride to a regional university to play football. That particular football player ended up having one too many drinks and physically assaulted his current girlfriend. Someone at the party ended up calling the cops and he was taken to jail that night. His parents bailed him out the next day and tried to hide the incident as well as they could.

He risked a whole lot on those drinks that night. His girlfriend could have been hurt much worse, and he could have lost that football scholarship. When I think about that night I feel very sad. I feel sad for the girl who was affected by her boyfriend's decisions that night. I feel sad for the football player who decided alcohol was more important to him than another human being's life. There is a way to have fun without alcohol. I promise!!! You can find people in whatever school you go to who do not want to participate in those things either. Do not buy into the lie that society tells us. You do not have to drink or smoke or party in order to have fun. Don't believe me? Come to my house...I'll show you how it is done!

Paul explains essentially what I am trying to get across to you in Ephesians 4:22-24. He says, "You were taught, in regard to your former way of life, to put off your old self, which is being corrupted by its deceitful desires; to be made new in the attitude of your minds; and to put on the new self, created to be like God in true righteousness and holiness." Unfortunately, we live in a world that is surrounded by the lies of the devil, especially in high school. You may hear things like, "If you don't drink you can't come." You may even hear things like, "You can't come hang out with us if you aren't going to smoke." Here's the thing. Those people are not your true friends. If they value what you will DO over who you ARE and what you stand for, that's a huge problem. I'm sure that if these kinds of conversations come up in your friend group you may feel pretty lonely, right? Here is some great news...The prophet Isaiah says in Isaiah 26:4, "Trust in the Lord forever, for the Lord, the Lord, is the Rock eternal." Now what do you think of when you hear the word "rock?" (Dwayne Johnson is not an acceptable answer.) I know that I think of words like "hard," "solid," and "firm." One of the definitions for the word *rock* is "a firm foundation or support." That is what the Lord is for you! If you allow Him, He will be your foundation and support through the hardest times. He will be with you at that party when you are tempted to do things you know are not pleasing to Him. He will also be with you when you decide not to do the things you are tempted to do and you are left feeling lonely and unwanted. Isaiah also says later on in Isaiah 41:13, "For I am the Lord, your God, who takes hold of your right hand and says to you, 'Do not fear; I will help you.'" Joshua 1:9 says, "Have I not commanded you? Be strong and courageous. Do not be terrified; do not be discouraged for the Lord, your God will be with you wherever you go."

What an awesome God we have. He leaves us with the promise to hold our hand and help us. We have His promise and, trust me, His promises are true. I know how hard it is to resist temptation in times like these. I totally understand. That beer is being handed to you by the quarterback of the football team. It is understandable that you want to take it and be just like everyone else. That is when you hold up your Coca-Cola can and say, "I'm good, thanks!" Stand firm ladies. He is with us.

Make School Social

Wait a minute; you're telling me that it is possible to have a social life in the midst of trying to maintain good grades? Yes! I am telling you just that! Your social life should come second to your schoolwork but it is possible to have one. During my freshman and sophomore years of high school I was not very involved in my school. I had a few friends, those two years, that I would hang out with on the weekends but aside from that, I didn't do much. I became more involved my junior year. With a little push, from a lot of people, I decided to run for junior class treasurer. I worked hard on my posters and prepared to give my speech. Sadly, I did not win the election. I was defeated and convinced that I would never run again. My mom, being the incredible woman she is, continued to encourage me and put the idea back in my mind. She told me that I had always had strong leadership abilities and she wanted to see that flourish in my high school. I really did want to run again, but I was scared. What if I lose again? I didn't want to be embarrassed! Believe it or not, I ran again my senior year. It took a lot of courage and preparation, but I am now my school's senior class treasurer. Deciding to run again was one of the best decisions I have ever made.

The atmosphere, of my small (400 students) charter high school, is very family-like and intentionally both loving and challenging. Believe it or not, we don't even have a school building. We go to school in portables! I absolutely love the set up. Everyone goes outside during class changes and for lunch. Who cares about the rain? We embrace it. The teachers at my school have always shown me that they cared about more than just my GPA. They care about their students as individuals instead of looking at them as only students. Of course, there are exceptions because no school is perfect. However, I must say, my high school is pretty dang close to perfect. One of the greatest teachers I have ever had to this day is a 30-something-year-old man who has one of the kindest hearts, wisest minds, and the most sarcastic of attitudes. Mr. Stone will be my homie forever for the way he cared about me all throughout high school. I would not trade my experience there for the world. Student government is a special place at my school, to say the least. My absolute best friends are my fellow student body officers. We are like one big family when we all get together! We even call our advisors Mama Bailey and Mama Meyers. In the fall of 2016 our student body held a "spirit week" and raised the most money our school had ever raised. Through that spirit week, specifically, I grew so much closer to not just my fellow student body officers, but my other classmates as well. It was such an exciting, emotional, thrilling experience. I remember the night of our final event. We revealed the amount of money we raised that week and the tears started flowing.

> ## What do you think it would look like to get involved in your high school?
>
> "Getting involved in sports!!"
>
> **Virginia - 7th Grader**
>
> "Getting to know everyone and trying to be very social!"
>
> **Lucy - 7th Grader**

Student government is just one of the many ways in which you can get involved in your school. Being a part of different clubs your school may offer is another great way! How about sports? How about different organizations within your school? Every school is different and every school has its own activities in which you can get involved! One thing I would challenge you to do in anything you end up getting involved in, is to be a leader. Now, you already are leaders. You may be followers. It doesn't matter which you would classify yourself as. The fact of the matter is you have the ability to lead your peers in positive uplifting ways that point back to Jesus.

My sophomore year, our student body president was one of the most incredible men I have ever met. He loved the Lord with all his heart and that showed in everything he did and through the way he interacted with the rest of the school. I have seen four different student body presidents in my time in high school. Some were incredible leaders, some were not. Some were positive influences, some were not. That is going to be true no matter where you end up going to high school. There will be those kinds of people in whatever you decide to become involved. You have the power to decide what kind of leader, friend, and student you wish to be.

This is a great opportunity. Don't waste it, girl. Keep your ears and eyes open to new possibilities and new opportunities within your school. Jesus may just be calling you to something you never imagined. Now that is something to be excited about.

Community is a great gift that the Lord has given us. Can you tell that I believe community is an important topic? This is the third time I have talked about it because it is just that important! Hebrews 10:24 says, "And let us consider how we may spur on one another on toward love and good deeds." You do not have to be student body president to have this power. You can be a positive leader wherever you decide to get involved! I hope you hear me say that. Jesus didn't pick society's most important people to become leaders. He used some average people and some of the lowest of the low in society during His time to help spread His word. Acts 4:13 says, "When they saw the courage of Peter and John and realized that they were unschooled, ordinary men, they were astonished and they took note that these men had been with Jesus." How crazy is that? Peter and John were two of Jesus' disciples, the men who followed Jesus throughout his entire ministry. They were "unschooled, ordinary men" that Jesus used for His purpose and His kingdom. Peter and John weren't kings or anyone high up in society. No. They were ordinary people like you and like me.

All throughout the Bible, Jesus has a habit of using the men and women to strengthen His kingdom that most would not expect. Take Matthew for example. Matthew was a tax collector. Tax collectors were one of the most hated groups of people during the time of Jesus. They were liars and cheaters. They would cheat people out of their money and keep most of it for themselves. Matthew, who was later given the name Levi, ended up writing the first gospel in the New Testament. How cool is that? The gospels were written by some of Jesus' closest friends about His life and his ministry. Jesus used Matthew and his story to benefit His kingdom in the end.

Let's back up and think about Jesus' mother Mary. Mary was a nobody at the time Jesus was born. She was not the daughter of a king or anyone with great power and yet the Lord still chose her. The angel, Gabriel, came to Mary one day and said, "Greetings, you who are highly favored! The Lord is with you" (Luke 1:28). He goes on to tell her that she is going to have the Son of God in her womb, even though she was still a virgin!

She responds with, "I am the Lord's servant. May it be to me as you have said" (Luke 1:38). I'm sorry but can we talk about courage for a second here? Mary is pretty incredible, wouldn't you say? I can promise you that if that situation happened to me I would have reacted very differently.

You have the ability to lead in any situation you are in. You have the power, within you, to be a positive example for the people around you in your high school. As Spiderman's Uncle Ben once said, "With great power comes great responsibility." (Sorry I'm a little bit of a nerd.) Not only did Uncle Ben tell Spiderman that, Jesus tells us that as well in the gospel of Luke. Luke 12:48 says, "From everyone who has been given much, much will be demanded; and from the one who has been entrusted with much, much more will be asked."

If you are a follower of Christ I can imagine you've tasted and seen some pretty amazing things. Jesus has a way of showing Himself to us in the most unusual ways. You have been given much. The Lord gave us His Son to die on the cross for our sins. When you think about it that way, how could we not go and be witnesses for Him? He is honest with us in Luke by saying "...much will be demanded." He asks us to live our lives for Him. When you begin living your life for Him and with Him, His joy and life will shine through you. Trust me.

MY prayers for YOU: Meg's Declassified Social Survival Guide

To the girl who is struggling to find "a place" in her high school, I pray the Lord will show you the place that is just right for you. (I Thessalonians 5:14)

To the girl struggling with friendships, I pray the Lord will reveal to you that you will always have a friend in Him. (John 15:15)

To the girl struggling with peer pressure, I pray the Lord will give you strength. (Romans 12:2)

To the girl struggling with getting involved and putting herself out there, I pray the Lord will provide you with the community you have been searching for. (Galatians 6:2)

To the girl who is struggling to let go of the things of this world she knows are wrong, I pray the Lord will give you strength. (Deuteronomy 31:6)

There she is, ladies! THE Kaytlin Cook you have heard so much about. The most beautiful and the most kind. I praise Jesus every day for giving her to me.

My Student Government family (AKA the greatest people ever!) Take a leap of faith if you feel like Student Government is something you would want to pursue. I would do it all over again in a heartbeat.

7

Bless the Lord, Oh My Soul

Jesus is...

Jesus and I have had a roller coaster relationship. There have been times I felt so close to Him and there have been times I have wondered if He even still existed. When you think of Jesus what do you think? You can ask a room of 100 people that question and you will probably get 100 different answers. The fact of the matter is that Jesus has many characteristics. The real question is why does this matter?

It all starts with understanding that Jesus is the visible image of the invisible God. Jesus is God in the flesh. Colossians 1:15-18 says, "The Son is the image of the invisible God, the firstborn over all creation. For in him all things were created: things in heaven and on earth, visible and invisible, whether thrones or powers or rulers or authorities; all things have been created through him and for him. He is before all things, and in him all things hold together." That is a lot to swallow, I understand, but this is good stuff, friend! This is why the different characteristics of Jesus are so important. This is why we need to look upon Jesus every day of our lives. Because when we clearly know and see the person of Jesus Christ, we see God the Father. As we see how Jesus lived and treated people, we understand how our Heavenly Father feels about us. He is crazy about us.

He delights in us. Jesus unveils the extravagant love of God for us. That truth changes everything.

Why did Jesus come to earth? Why did Jesus come down from Heaven to be a part of a broken and sinful world? Jesus did this to show us a visible image of God and to take away the sin of the world. He did this to save us from ourselves and to forever change history. The characteristics that Jesus possesses would mean nothing if sin had not been taken away. John 1:14 says, "The Word became flesh and made his dwelling among us. We have seen his glory, and the glory of the one and only Son, who came from the Father, full of grace and truth." The Word became flesh so He could be a part of our world and dwell among us. Jesus is our everlasting friend, healer, and strength. All these sides of Jesus are good and perfect. They affect our lives in different ways and at different times. Jesus' characteristics show up in diverse situations and in different times of our lives. I want to show you four characteristics of Jesus that have been very present in my life throughout my years of middle school and high school just to give you a glimpse of Jesus' character. (Which is also God the Father's character, in case you didn't get that earlier!!!)

Who is Jesus to you?

"He is a pretty awesome dude. The one that died on the cross to forgive us of our sins. Life has thrown me lots of curve balls throughout high school and never once has He left my side."

Katie - High School Senior

Jesus is my strength. Psalm 28:7 says, "The Lord is my strength and my shield; my heart trusts in him, and he helps me." I battled many lies during my teenage years. I struggled to believe that I was pretty enough, skinny enough, worthy enough, and overall good enough. After Jack and I broke up, these lies took control of my life. I struggled to believe that I would ever be the same. I struggled to believe that I could ever be redeemed. Choosing to change those lies to true statements that I believed about myself was painfully difficult. It took some serious restructuring of my thought process and it was hard! Jesus was there through it all. Jesus held me in His arms and allowed me to see myself in a new light. He placed people in my life to help guide and protect me through the entire process.

Jesus is my friend. John 15:15 says, "I no longer call you servants, because a servant does not know his master's business. Instead, I have called you friends, for everything that I have learned from my Father I have made known to you." For me, when I was in middle school, I struggled with friendships. I was caught in the middle of very hard and very hurtful situations and I struggled to believe that anyone would want to be my friend. I wondered what was wrong with me to make no one want to be my friend. During that time, Jesus showed me that He was my friend. Jesus showed me that He wanted to hear about my day, my fears, my failures, my worries, and the things that interested me. I fell in love with that side of Jesus and I honestly believed that's what drew me most to Him during my time in middle school.

Jesus is my healer. Isaiah 53:5 says, "But he was pierced for our transgressions, he was crushed for our iniquities; the punishment that brought us peace was on him. And by his wounds we are healed." I don't know about you but those words hit the spot for me. I know that for a very long time I believed I would never heal from the wounds I had experienced; some inflicted on me and some I brought on myself. I believed that my past could never be made new. Isaiah proves me wrong every time. (Seriously, Isaiah is awesome!) Jesus died the worst death in human history because He couldn't stand the fact that I felt that way. He gave Himself as a living sacrifice so I could be healed from my wounds, from my past, from my failures, and from my future mistakes. Here's the deal: He feels that way about you as well. He has healed us forever and that, my friend, is one beautiful story.

Jesus is everlasting. Hebrews 13:8 says, "Jesus Christ is the same yesterday and today and forever." We have all experienced temporary joy in this world. It could be as shallow as the temporary joy of drinking a milkshake and then the sadness of finishing it off at some point. It could be as deep as the joy of making a new friend followed by the sadness of a falling out for some unknown reason. The things of this world are not eternal. Hebrews shows us that Jesus is the only constant figure in our lives. Some days it may feel like Jesus is very far from you. You may feel like Jesus doesn't have control of the situations going on in your life and if He did have control, then why is He allowing them to happen? Jesus' love is everlasting. Jesus' friendship, His strength, and His ability to heal us every day is constant and everlasting. In this truth, we can have peace. That peace comes from knowing that when all the things of this world fail you, Jesus will be there to catch you and help you back to your feet.

> *If you could leave a note of encouragement to a middle school girl about faith and Jesus what would it be?*
>
> "Stay in touch (with Jesus). It will help you I promise. I have learned that being in a relationship with God has taken some stress off of me."
>
> **Margaret - High School Freshman**

I encourage you, as you grow in your relationship with Jesus, to begin recognizing His characteristics as He reveals them to you. When we recognize the characteristics of Jesus, we are recognizing the character of God. The One who delights in us, the One who loves us, and the One who is our everlasting friend, healer, and strength is waiting for you, with open arms, to look to Him and say, "Reveal yourself to me, Lord Jesus. I need you." I promise you, He will answer.

The Best Book

The summer after my sophomore year of high school I went backpacking for a week. There is a Young Life camp in Creede, Colorado called Wilderness Ranch. I found that the sheer excitement (and terror) of being in the middle of the mountains for a week with some of your closest friends and Young Life leaders was an exhilarating experience. Now, going into this trip, I knew nothing about hiking. My grandfather, who genuinely enjoys the outdoors, had generously given me some books he thought would be useful for me to read pre-trip. If I am honest I still had no idea what I was getting myself into and had no clue what the week would be like. Fortunately, our guides had some idea what to expect and packed the necessary tools and equipment for our trek. The journey was one I will never forget. We hiked from Sunday to Friday. Wednesday was what our guides called "peak day." Peak day was supposed to be the most exhilarating day of the whole trip. Our peak day, however, was not. Our guides woke us up super early that morning and we put on all of our hiking gear, strapped on our backpacks, and set off for the peak. Or so we thought.

We began hiking and, to our surprise, we saw snow, lots and lots of snow. The group of us from the South was excited at first glance because we don't see a lot of snow. Plus who doesn't love a good snow, right? The further up the path we walked the more snow we came into contact with. The snow started coming down pretty fast and we were walking in at least 10 inches of snow. (In hiking shorts I might add. The picture I'm including was taken during the "YAY snow!" phase of the day when it hadn't gotten deep yet). The hour and a half we walked through the snow was the worst hour and a half of my life. My toes were totally frozen; I was shaking uncontrollably and was wondering how we were ever going to get out of the mess we were in.

All 14 of us were crying and our guides, I could tell, were genuinely concerned. White ground was ahead of us and white ground was behind us. Suddenly we saw a small patch of grass with a stream running through it. I kid you not when I say this was a random patch of grass in the middle of a blizzard. I have no doubt that Jesus put it there just for us. Our guides kept telling us that if we could just get to that patch we would stop and decide what to do next. We pushed forward. With each step in the snow my toes grew colder and my legs felt heavier. We made it to the patch of grass and unloaded our gear.

Do you remember those big parachutes you played with in kindergarten? You and all your friends take a side of it and flip it upward as hard as you could and then you all sit on it underneath to keep the air inside. That is what we had to do. Our guides pulled out our "emergency shelter" and we all pitched in to create our parachute. We all sat inside, on the edges of the parachute and were warmed by the carbon dioxide we were exhaling. I have never been more scared in my life. We all looked at each other and began to cry out to the Lord. We begged Him to make clear to us what the best course of action would be. We began passing around soggy coffee cake and apple slices that our guides found in someone's pack. Sadly, we made the decision, with our guides, to turn around and head back, through all the snow we had just come through. We would not be able to make the peak after all.

Looking back at that day now, I laugh. Two of our girls came home with frostbite but it's fine - everyone has ten toes and ten fingers, don't worry! When I look at the bigger picture of what actually went down that day, I realize that there is no way we would have survived, unharmed, without the proper tools. We had our guides, we had our emergency shelter, we had food and we had each other's CO_2 to keep us warm. Without the proper tools, we would have been doomed in the actual wilderness.

When you hear the words "The Bible" what do you think? Some words that pop into my head are "long", "intimidating", "confusing," "boring," and maybe even "scary." I think the most important thing to remember about the Bible is that it is a tool. I shared with you a bit about my backpacking trip. We would not have survived the way we did without the proper tools. The Bible is our tool to navigating life without our guide, Jesus, physically walking right next to us every day. Now, I totally understand that reading the Bible can be pretty scary. I have asked myself many times while reading, "Why on earth am I doing this?" The answer is found in Psalm 119:105. "Your word is a lamp to my feet and a light for my path." David, the author of many of the Psalms, is essentially saying without the Bible as our guide, we are walking through this life blindfolded. How do we know what is right and wrong? How do we know what the heck we are to do with our lives? Psalm 119:11 tells us, "I have hidden your word in my heart that I might not sin against you."

In "hiding" the Lord's words for us in our hearts, we become enriched with His spirit and His plan for our lives. James 1:22 says, "Do not merely listen to the word, and so deceive yourself. Do what it says." James makes a very good point. If I am honest, I struggle with treating my Bible reading a lot like a chore to check off of my checklist instead of looking at it as a life guide, if you will. I fail often to acknowledge the fact that this book was meant for me to live my everyday life by. I sometimes even overlook the things that I may not want to work on in my life. Reading the Bible is hard, I totally understand. But the reward and the connection you form with Jesus through His word, is unbeatable.

"All Scripture is God-breathed and is useful for teaching, rebuking, correcting and training in righteousness..." 2 Timothy 3:16

Faith with Feet

The summer after my junior year of high school, I was given an incredible opportunity. I was given the opportunity to serve at one of Young Life's most private camp properties in, wait for it, the beautiful British Columbia, Canada! The camp is called Malibu Club. I could talk to you for hours about my time spent at Malibu. I can honestly say that I have never worked so hard in my entire life. We were always running around setting tables, serving meals, doing dishes, setting up for the next event and whatever else we were needed to do in order for camp to run smoothly. My friends and I were called the "work crew." Work crew is an old school Young Life term that has been around for forever and honestly does a solid job of explaining the experience. We worked. We worked so very hard during those four weeks. But we were also a crew. The other high school students I was working alongside became my best friends. I learned more about myself in those four weeks than I have my entire life.

I came out of that month with new friendships that I know I will cherish forever and ever. The entire time we spent at Malibu we were actively serving. Now, I hate to use that word because I feel like in today's world it has become a very "churchy" word. However, I cannot get around using it in this situation because that is exactly what we did all month. We were serving with our time, our bodies, and with our minds. As strange as that sounds, it's true. I was physically and mentally exhausted at the end of every day. I had to learn what active serving looked like within that setting. Young Life needs the work crew because honestly, without them, camp could not operate the way it does. The whole purpose of Young Life camping is to introduce high school students to the extravagant love Jesus has for them. Part of that is shown through the work crew.

I learned something very important during my time at Malibu. I learned that my faith has to have feet in order for it to flourish. Now, what do I mean by this? Great question! Once you are in a relationship with Jesus this new desire will be put in your heart. That desire will cause you to want to share the love of Jesus that you have experienced with those around you. You will feel it, I promise. I also promised you earlier that we would discuss this topic later on, and here we are! One of the most tangible ways to do this is through serving others because when we serve, we are showing a clear picture of God's love for us and for others.

Mark 10:45 says, "For even the Son of Man did not come to be served, but to serve, and to give his life as a ransom for many." God's only Son came to earth, not to bring Himself glory upon glory, but to serve His people and to eventually give His life away.

> *Is faith an important factor in your everyday decision making process and why?*
>
> "Yes! (Faith) will keep you from making wrong or bad decisions."
>
> **Emily - 7th Grader**
>
> "Yes! Trusting God has played a huge role in me staying sane during high school. I am thankful to those who shared a Bible verse with me in a tough time or took a moment to pray with me. And returning the favor to someone else in need feeds your soul in such an amazing way."
>
> **Natalie - High School Senior**

John 13 is an incredible chapter in the Bible that shares the story of Jesus washing His disciples' feet. I am going to give you a little context on this story just to get you thinking. In Jesus' day, there were no paved roads. Every road was made of dirt and grass. Also, fashion had not progressed far enough along by this time for Nike tennis shoes to be a staple in everyone's wardrobe. Everyone walked places wearing open-toed sandals. So their feet got pretty dusty and dirty. It was customary for people to wash their feet before entering someone else's home. The servants of the household were normally the ones who washed the feet of the guests. For Jesus to get on His knees and wash His disciples' feet was completely absurd. Verse 6 says, "He came to Simon Peter, who said to him, 'Lord, are you going to wash my feet?' Jesus replied, 'You do not realize now what I am doing, but later you will understand.'" You see, Peter did not understand that Jesus was choosing to make Himself "less than" in the name of service. We serve because our faith has to have feet! Jesus doesn't need you to serve, but He does want you to.

Living a faith with feet is no simple task, but it is a choice we are given. There were definitely days when I woke up in Malibu, where the last thing I wanted to do was get up and go serve high school kids their breakfast. There were days all I wanted to do was sleep. I had to make a choice every day I was there to sacrifice my wants for the benefit of someone else. I learned something else very valuable while at Malibu. I learned that service is beautiful. The cover of this book is a painting of a picture I took off of the deck at Malibu. It was during my time there that I really felt like the Lord was calling me to pursue writing this book. Naturally, I had to put it on the cover. Malibu is beautiful, yes, it definitely is. But the service we were doing while we were there was more beautiful than the scenery itself. I experienced more community, more joy, and more freedom in giving my life away for others than I had felt any other time of my life. When I think back to my month at Malibu, I don't just remember the beautiful scenery. I remember the people I was serving with every day. I remember the perseverance we had as a work crew. I remember the life change I had the pleasure of witnessing in hundreds of high school students. Philippians 2:3-4 says, "Do nothing out of selfish ambition or vain conceit. Rather, in humility value others above yourselves, not looking to your own interests but each of you to the interest of others." That, my friends, is the way Jesus lived His life here on earth, and that is the most beautiful service of all.

Now, you could very possibly be thinking right now, "Where and how can people my age actively serve?" That is a very fair question to be pondering. It is a hard question to answer as well, so I am right there with you. I believe that Jesus has created many outlets in which you can serve. I feel like when people hear the word "serve" they think of missions in third world countries. As true as this may be, that is not all that service can be. I know that getting on a plane right this second and flying to Africa to share the Gospel with others is not a possibility for everyone. The fact of the matter is, going downstairs right now and doing the dishes for your mom is an act of service. Helping your little sibling with his or her homework is another way you can serve within your own family. Service does not have to be in a different country in order for it to make a difference in someone's life. Serving in your local church could be another great opportunity for the Lord to use you. Our faith has got to have feet or it will not flourish.

The band Casting Crowns released a song recently with their new album that I absolutely love. The song is called What If I Gave Everything. One of the verses in this song is so beautiful and so true that I had to share it with you:

> So why am I still standing here?
> Why am I still holding back from You?
> You've given me a faith that can move mountains
> But I'm still playing in the sand
> Building little kingdoms that'll never stand
> I hear you call me out into deeper waters
> But I settle on the shallow end
> I'm so tired of standing here...[1]

He is calling your name! He wants to use you and your story for incredible things that will benefit his kingdom. I hope that you will live your life, not just in high school but every day, out of that truth and use the feet that your faith has.

I have mentioned three things that I believe to be vitally important to remember as you walk with the Lord though your high school years and beyond. However, there is one other area I wish to think about with you and that is this; the local church. Learning the characteristics of Jesus, engaging in the Word, and living a faith with feet is impossible to do on your own. That is why the Lord gave us fellow believers and the local church. Fellow believers in the church are there to walk through this journey with us. They are there to guide us and they are there to help us. Ephesians 3:10-11 says, "His intent was that now, through the church, the manifold wisdom of God should be made known to the rulers and authorities in the heavenly realms, according to his eternal purpose that he accomplished in Christ Jesus our Lord." You see, the church was made to be a safe place for you and for me where the Lord teaches us more about Himself. No one church is perfect. Because the church is made up of humans, like you and me, that means it is made up of broken people. Regardless of your history or personal experience in the church, whether that be positive, negative, or no experience at all, I would encourage you to continue to search for one in your area. The church can be a place that will challenge you spiritually as well as personally through community. Searching for a place where you are able to learn more about the One who pursues you each and every day sounds like a great idea to me.

My Prayers for YOU: Bless the Lord, O my Soul!

For the girl who feels like she has nothing to offer, I pray that you will know and understand that the Lord has plans to use you in mighty ways. (Philippians 2:13)

For the girl who feels like there is no way she could ever get through a chapter of the Bible, I pray the Lord puts people in your life that will encourage you and help you find answers. (Psalm 119:130)

For the girl who is struggling to see the different characteristics of Jesus in her own life, I pray that the Lord will reveal Himself to you so clearly in the coming years. (Isaiah 41:10)

For the girl who is struggling to believe that Jesus would even want to use her to strengthen His kingdom, I pray that you will see and believe that your story has the potential to make an impact! (Proverbs 3:5)

Wilderness Ranch holds such a special place in my heart. I thank Jesus for the memories and stories that came out of that week!

This picture was taken while we still had the "YAYYY SNOW" attitude. The farther we hiked, the quicker that attitude went away

Conclusion

One of my favorite passages in the Bible comes from Luke 5. In this chapter, there is a story of a man with leprosy. Leprosy is a horrible disease that was very common during Jesus' time on earth. Leprosy affects a person's skin and leaves sores all over the body. It is spread through human contact. During the time of Jesus, anyone who had leprosy was considered "unclean" and was avoided at all cost. No one touched these people. No one came anywhere near these people. They were normally pushed to the outskirts of a city and essentially told to fend for themselves. In this passage, a man with leprosy saw Jesus and exclaimed, "'Lord if you are willing, you can make me clean.' Jesus reached out his hand and touched the man. 'I am willing,' he said. 'Be clean!' And immediately the leprosy left him" (Luke 5:13). What Jesus did in this situation was unheard of at the time. I want you to notice a key picture that I love about this passage. Jesus reached out and touched this man BEFORE he was healed. He touched the man BEFORE He did anything else. Jesus could have very easily just said, "be clean" in passing and not bothered to physically interact with this man whatsoever. I imagine this man was on the ground, his only possession a mat to sit on, with his arms outstretched begging for Jesus. Jesus came down to the man and touched his skin; the skin that was covered in a contagious disease that was considered "unclean."

Girlfriend, as you enter high school, I pray that you will be able to remember that Jesus Christ is willing to get down on the mat with you. He is willing to touch you, even if you are covered in sores and think you have nowhere to turn. He is waiting for you with arms stretched wide. He didn't tell this man, "Get rid of your leprosy then come to me." No! He got down on the mat with the man and He healed him. When you find yourself on your mat, defeated, on the outskirts of town, hurt, and feeling "unclean", I pray that you will invite Jesus into your mess. He is not ashamed of you and He wants to be with you. He wants to be a part of your life and He wants to be involved in your mess. He doesn't want you to try and clean yourself up and then come to Him. He wants you just the way you are, mess and all. I promise you. I got myself into many messes during my high school years that left me with a lot of sores. I struggled to comprehend that there was a God who wanted anything to do with me. But He did and He still does. And guess what? He wants you too! He wants you to invite Him in, even when you feel like He doesn't want to be there. I am a firm believer that if I had not humbled myself and asked Jesus to heal me when I did, I would not be where I am today. Learn from my mistakes. He is ready and willing to heal you, because trust me, you cannot do it yourself.

Through reading the pages of this book, you have seen a glimpse of what life was like for me in middle school and high school. Things were not always easy; I will be the first to admit that. You have read my personal thoughts, the thoughts of your peers, and the thoughts of other high school girls and I hope that they have challenged you to think further on the seven topics mentioned. I do not want you to enter high school thinking you will not make a single mistake, because you will. I also do not want you to enter high school thinking you have already made too many mistakes to try anything different. You have a great opportunity to have a fresh start that begins your very first day of high school, freshman year. As soon as you step out of the car door on your first day, you have an opportunity to do things differently. I wanted to close this book by sharing a passage of the Bible with you that is very near and dear to my heart. I mentioned earlier how Isaiah is my favorite book in the Bible. Chapter 43 means so much to me and I wanted to share it with you today.

[1]"But now, this is what the LORD says—
he who created you, Jacob,
he who formed you, Israel:
"Do not fear, for I have redeemed you;
I have summoned you by name; you are mine.

[2] When you pass through the waters,
I will be with you;
and when you pass through the rivers,
they will not sweep over you.
When you walk through the fire,
you will not be burned;
the flames will not set you ablaze....

[4] Since you are precious and honored in my sight,
and because I love you,
I will give people in exchange for you,
nations in exchange for your life.
[5] Do not be afraid, for I am with you;

This passage shows us two things: who we are and who the Lord is. Verse 4 says very clearly who you are, friend. You are "precious and honored." You are His. You are worth dying for. Those are the truths I pray you will carry on through your high school years. The Lord is your Creator and your Redeemer. No matter what may happen or what kind of curve balls get thrown your way, He is always there. He is more than willing to get down on the mat and be involved in your pain and in your success. He is willing to touch your sores and heal you in ways you can never imagine. Now, it's your turn to go. Go into your high school with the security that you have a God who is on your side rooting for you, every day of your life. He has been there from the beginning and He won't abandon you; not now, not ever. So, you have heard my story and you have heard the words that that the Lord has for you. Now it is your turn. Girlfriend, you got this!

Things to look forward to in high school...

Prom ...

College Searching ...

School Sporting Events ...

School Dances and Events ...

Notes:

All Scripture quotations, unless otherwise noted, are taken from the New International Version of the Bible, published in 1978.

chapter three: Boys, Boys, Boys

1. Gresh, Dannah. What Are You Waiting For?. WaterBrook Publishing, 2012

2. Chart adapted from Dennis and Barbara Rainey's Passport 2 Purity, published by FamilyLife Publishing.

3. West, Matthew. "Mended."

chapter four: beYOUtiful

1. Explanations adapted from "Women's Body Image and BMI: Look at the evolution of the female figure over 100 years," Rehabs.com, http://www.rehabs.com/explore/womens-body-image-and-bmi/

2. Rivers, Francine. Redeeming Love. Multnomah Books Publishing, 1989.

3. Holcomb, Ellie. "Wonderfully Made."

chapter seven: Bless the Lord, O my Soul!

1. Crowns, Casting. "Why am I Still Standing Here?"

About the Author

Megan Bokowy, a high school senior out of Greenville, South Carolina, is thrilled to promote Surviving the Wild: A Girlfriend's Guide to High School as her first ever book. Megan loves the

freedom and redemption found in living life with Jesus and wishes to share that love with middle school girls through this book. She plans to attend a four-year university next year to study political science with the hope of eventually attending law school. When Megan is not in school or working at the beloved Chick-Fil-A, you will more than likely find her at the closest Starbucks with a group of friends or with her family at a Young Life camp!

Photo by Lucy Chapman Photography
lucyphoto.com

To order additional copies or to personally contact Megan, please use the email, megansguide101@gmail.com.

You can also follow Megan on her social media platforms by using the handle @megan_bokowy.

additional resources

I have found that the Lord uses different outlets in order to speak to our hearts. For me, I have heard Him speak to me through books and through music. I wanted to include a few book titles and musical artists that I have found to be very encouraging and uplifting to me through my high school years! I hope that you will find them to be just as encouraging. I pray that you will know the One who gave His life for you and the One who delights in you is always waiting for you with open arms. He loves you and wants you to hear His voice. Listen for it.

Books:

Redeeming Love by Francine Rivers
Love Does by Bob Goff
And the Bride Wore White by Danna Gresh
What are You Waiting For? by Danna Gresh
Living the Cross Centered Life by CJ Mahaney
Free to be Me by Stasi Eldredge
Jesus Calling by Sarah Young
The Screwtape Letters by CS Lewis
The Chronicles of Narnia by C.S. Lewis

Music:

Ellie Holcomb
Casting Crowns
Matthew West
NEEDTOBREATHE
Tenth Avenue North
MercyMe
Laura Story
Scott Cash
Ben Rector
Tim Halperin

72556008R00060